What People are Saying about
GETTING *thru* TO KIDS

"A cohesive new approach to effective communication with children."

- Patrick Wyatt, School Psychologist, M.F.C.C.

"This book is a fine contribution to the 'science' of communication. Guiding adults through 'win,win' dialogues with children, Phillip Mountrose does much to enhance the self-esteem and dignity of both the adult and the child.

- Barbara Silver, Principal

"I have found the book's strategies to be powerful and effective, fostering respect between adult and child. It's a unique resource!"

- Margaret Messina, Special Education Teacher

"Adults can get stuck in their own reactions and actually reinforce negative behavior in children. The steps mapped out by Phillip Mountrose can change those reactions into positive behavior reinforcement for both adult and child."

- Karen Knutsen Johnson, Clinical Hypnotherapist

"I usually take control without giving my daughter a chance to express how she feels and find out what's on her mind. The 5 Steps allowed me to be more patient and stay calm. I thought about how I can include her in figuring out the solution, rather than 'daddy' figuring it out or doing it.... It gives her a chance to grow and understand."

- Gerald Rainey, parent

"It was easier to talk with him. This time I get to explain my part. He listened better."
- Dominique Rainey, age 9, Gerald's daughter

"My children will come to their own solutions through this 5 Step Approach. They will be more likely to try it than if I say 'do this'.... Actually they came up with better solutions to their problems than I did, which surprised me. They were able to think of solutions that are very workable!"
- Bernice Lunsford, parent

"My mom was more calm. She made me think how I was bored and how to fix it. I think I'll solve more of my own problems now."
- Brandon Lunsford, age 11, Bernice's son

"This time mom gave us more help. It's easier than the way we used to solve problems."
- Amber Lunsford, age 12, Bernice's daughter

"This approach taught me to listen and search out my daughter's feelings. The approach was very simple, just to listen and know what to ask and look for. I will try it any time she has a problem, big or small, so I can see what's really bothering her.... Communication is the key to everybody's well-being." - Diana Louis, parent

"I had a chance to speak my mind more, which is a lot different. We resolved the problem. I think the process is good for parent and daughter or son."
- Mindy Louis, age 17, Diana's daughter

"I can gain more empathy on how my son's thinking because he's part of the problem-solving. He'll be more willing to go with the parameters we come up with.

He's going to be more receptive. It teaches independence, problem-solving, and self-esteem. I think it's terrific."
                                      - Duane Simpfenderfer, parent

"I notice my daughter is calmer. She's more in control of her feelings. Our communication is a whole lot better."
                                      - Barbie Morgan, parent

"We got more ideas. It feels better because there are a lot of ways we can try them.... I'd rather have both of us problem solve."
                         - Stephanie Morgan, age 9, Barbie's daughter

"I naturally talk more, listen less. This time I sat down and wanted to hear what he had to say. Children are smarter than we give them credit for. They can come up with solutions themselves if we give them a chance.... They feel included."
                                      -Punam Kaura, parent

"My mother was calmer and open to new ideas. It makes me feel better that I came up with the solution all by myself."
                         - Vishal Kaura, age 14, Punam's son

"I felt it was easier to talk with my son about his problems. He usually doesn't talk too much... I think it will lead to trusting in me and coming to me with any problem. And when he gets older and has his own family, he will know how to talk with them about their problems.... I am grateful I learned this process."
                                      - Kimberly Johnson, parent

Book and Cover Design
by Jane Mountrose

GETTING *thru* TO KIDS

Problem Solving with Children Ages 6 to 18

Phillip Mountrose

Holistic Communications
Sacramento, California

Published by: Holistic Communications
                 P.O. Box 41152
                 Sacramento, CA 95841-0152 USA
                 Fax: 916-972-0237, E-mail: getthru@jps.net

ISBN: 0-9653787-7-2
Library of Congress Catalog Card Number: 96-95358

Publisher's Cataloging in Publication
    (Prepared by Quality Books Inc.)
Mountrose, Phillip.
Getting thru to kids: problem solving with children
ages 6 to 18 / Phillip Mountrose.
p. cm.
Includes biographical references and index.
ISBN 0-9653787-7-2
1. Problem solving in children. 2. Child rearing. 3. Parenting.
I. Title.
BF723.P8M68 1997   155.4'13
                                  QB196-2563

ATTENTION COLLEGES AND UNIVERSITIES, CORPORATIONS AND PROFESSIONAL ORGANIZATIONS: Quantity discounts are available on bulk purchases of this book for educational training purposes, fund raising or gift giving. Special books, booklets or book excerpts can also be created to fit your specific needs. For information contact publisher.

Table of Contents

In Appreciation

To my wife Jane, who is a terrific companion, teacher and support in my life. To the suggestions and input by Sandy Rhymer, Barbara Silver, Margaret Messina, Judy Hansen, Marion Hakata, and Troy Valentine. To Jeffrey Lant for his insightful how-to books. And to my parents for their love and support. I also thank every one who tried to get through to me.

Introduction

THE ESSENCE OF THIS BOOK AND HOW IT CAN HELP YOU

Did you know that 6,000 school-age children die from homicide or suicide each year? *"The most common identified motive was a dispute* [my italics]. This could have been interpersonal, romantic, one over money or property or over a sporting event," according to Dr. Gail Stennies of the Centers for Disease Control and Prevention.

Maybe you're not involved with suicidal or homicidal kids. But just think how many daily misunderstandings with kids occur that create a host of stressful problems. These difficulties can range from annoyances to abuse and violence.

My aim in this work is to give you specific, concrete ways to communicate and problem solve effectively with kids. The *Merriam Webster Dictionary* tells us to communicate means "to make known; to pass from one to another, transmit." This is a two way street between you and the child.

Getting Thru to Kids will empower you with the tools to handle kids' problems so they will in turn be more responsible for themselves. Young people will come to know their own thoughts and feelings. And unlike most available resources, this book shows you how to help children find the underlying cause of the problem. After helping them discover what generated the trouble in the first place, you will learn how to have kids naturally convert a gloomy outlook to a bright outlook.

This kind of communication helps your relationships with young people of all ages to become more trusting and lasting. It also raises everyone's self-esteem. You will discover that these benefits can grow over a lifetime for all involved.

WHAT YOU'LL FIND IN GETTING THRU TO KIDS

I would like to briefly introduce to you this volume's ten chapters and the six appendices.

Chapter 1 examines two approaches you have used... and how they can easily make matters worse for the kids you are trying to help. First, you will learn the limitations of an authoritarian, "do it or else" approach with children. Second, you will discover the shortcomings of an alternative approach that is based on rewarding kids for their behavior. By becoming more aware of what doesn't work, you are better prepared to learn what does.

Chapter 2 helps you avoid contributing to the growing statistics of abuse and violence in the country. As you become more aware of the downward cycle, you realize the need to consciously work with kids.

Chapter 3 gives you a specific method to problem solve with kids, empowering them to discover their own answers with you as a guide and resource. A 5-step process will take you from identifying the problem, working with feelings and thoughts, and then creating a new outlook and vision of the future. Through the process, the youngster develops his thinking abilities and takes more responsibility for himself. As you show the child you are more aware of him, he becomes more aware of himself and others.

Chapter 4 breaks down the 5-step problem solving process into more specifics for easier understanding and application.

Chapter 5 gives you the tools to confidently progress with kids through helping them solve their problems. It helps you to be calm and collected. You will discover how to change power struggles into communication breakthroughs. By learning five key communication skills, you will become a powerful communicator with children. In turn, this will help youngsters to help themselves.

Chapter 6 addresses your own personal needs and how they relate to children. You will find out how to identify what is important to you. Then you will know when and how to communicate your own needs and concerns to kids.

Chapter 7 puts what you have learned in the previous chapters together. You will find helpful transcriptions that demonstrate the 5-step problem solving process you learned in

Chapter 3. Included are key annotations so you will know the flow of the process and how you can fit it altogether.

Chapter 8 provides reference tips to guide you through the 5-step problem solving process. As you use this powerful approach, you can refer to this guide for troubleshooting and immediate solutions.

Chapter 9 will allow you to test out the process yourself, having a firsthand opportunity to see how it works and to reap the benefits of better communication.

Chapter 10 takes stock of the tools you have learned and how to apply them. It looks at the big picture. It examines how the communication ability you have developed can profoundly improve society as a whole.

The Appendices are further resources that help you:

- Identify the stages in child development so you can specifically help kids with their problems.

- Develop words that fit feelings, so children can better express their own feelings.

- Know different kinds of beliefs - ones that cause problems, ones that solve problems.

- Find examples of commonly held limiting and liberating beliefs.

- Use a guided visualization, empowering you and kids to transform problems.

- Become aware of your own thought processes and how they can restrict or liberate you. ، ..

WHERE I'M COMING FROM

I have been an educator for over twenty years, much of the time in special education. Working as a teacher with troubled kids and their parents, it became obvious that there was a need for better communication both in the classroom and in the home. It also became evident that there was a scarcity of role models and information showing adults how to help children mature into adulthood.

For the last six years, I have been teaching emotionally disturbed teenage boys, ages ten to eighteen. "Getting thru" is definitely a challenge. Nonetheless, I was drawn to the challenge, both to work with them and learn from them. Traditional methods of learning had already been tried - and failed - with these boys, so I knew I would have to be creative.

In the established school procedure, a student who became disruptive was directed to a time out area, away from others. The teacher or assistant talked with him after the boy calmed down. Even though the staff was compassionate and well-trained, something seemed missing in this procedure.

The time out discussion would usually start with a review of the problem. Then the adult asked the boy if he was willing to stop the misbehavior and cooperate with the program. The boy usually agreed, knowing he could not leave the time out area unless he said he would follow the rules. But nothing had really changed. The student still held the same thoughts and feelings about his problem. The results were external and the same problems generally recurred, to the frustration of all involved.

Behavior modification techniques like time outs are helpful and sometimes necessary with both normal and disturbed children. But without getting into the thoughts and feelings behind the behavior, true change is slow at best. In this way, children miss an opportunity to internalize the learning.

In fact, I noticed with my students that time outs could have a reverse effect. Since they were not able to express themselves, the youngsters often became increasingly resentful. The time outs reinforced their feelings of powerlessness and low esteem. Poor self-image was the reason they were disturbed in the first place. Most of them believed that life is unfair and they didn't fit in - the time outs just reinforced that.

During these years I continued to study various forms of psychology and alternative learning methods. I also drew from my own teaching experience. I investigated Cognitive Therapy that deals with belief systems and NLP (Neuro Linguistic Programming) which develops various communication skills. I studied with two powerful mentors, Barry Snyder and Karen Anderson, who helped me understand patterns of healing. By gaining this broader picture of human interactions, I mapped out a 5-step process for problem solving.

Amazingly, it worked. The boys began to speak more openly as they sensed someone was really listening. They shared their feelings, found new understandings and became problem solvers. Confidence lit up their expressions. I benefited, too. I became a better listener and nurturer. Where there once were walls, now there were windows and doors. It was wonderful! More light was shining in.

The method wasn't an instant cure-all, especially for emotionally disturbed boys. Lasting change is gradual. But if the process worked with them, I felt it could be even more effective with "normal" children, who are more stable. I shared this method with colleagues and parents and received encouraging feedback.

THE JOURNEY

You, too, have a journey that includes getting through to kids. After you have read this work and begun its application, I would appreciate hearing from you and the successes you have experienced. I like to know about fellow communicators. My address is in the back of this volume. I also can help you with individual situations involving kids. I congratulate you for investing in yourself and children. Your success will not only be a great benefit to you, but it will help many others who are in your life as well.

CHAPTER ONE

Starting Out Right ... and Wrong

If we are to reach real peace in this world...
we shall have to begin with the children.

--MAHATMA GANDHI

USING AUTHORITY WITHOUT BECOMING AN AUTHORITARIAN

Most people want to help kids with their problems, preparing them to be happy, responsible adults. This book presents some unique and effective ways to communicate that assist both the adult and the child. Unlike the traditional "do it or else" method of problem solving, which mostly creates fear and resentment, the child actively participates, learning skills that will help him or her throughout life.

Mastering the techniques requires an open mind and a little time, but the results speak for themselves. Even when you are just starting and don't have a complete grasp of the process, you and the child will notice a difference. As one mother put it, referring to her nine year old daughter:

"I used to problem solve with my children much differently, not seeing things from their perspective. Now I feel more respectful of my daughter. It took some of the load off of me. She took some of the responsibility. I never thought she could do that. I'm really happy getting that from the process. I feel she'll be more comfortable coming to me in the future. If one doesn't solve youth conflicts, they'll become adult conflicts. This process helps me identify the conflict when it's much more manageable."

It is standard practice to have training for virtually any profession. It is amazing, then, with all of the educational opportunities available today, most of us have not received any training in parenting, one of life's greatest challenges.

Adults often have great intentions, fueled by love and caring for children. But amidst daily challenges and stress, our approach resorts to hit and miss. We settle for muddling through, relying mostly on the ways our parents used, even though today's challenges are so different. In many cases, the old approach that our parents tried didn't work too well in the first place.

Perhaps in the future, the educational system will instruct young adults on how to raise children effectively. In the meantime, today's parents need to piece the puzzle together for themselves. The Getting Thru techniques provide some key pieces to this puzzle.

Getting Thru to Kids shifts away from simple obedience, the "do it or else" approach mentioned earlier. The participants take time to explore the thoughts and feelings about their problems. In turn, their thinking reveals beliefs that create unspoken rules by which they live. In many cases, these thought forms could be more accurately described as *limiting* beliefs, because they actually put up barriers to attaining our goals in life.

For instance, most of us know a person who believes that life is tough and somehow her experiences reflect that belief. Most of us also know a person who views life as an exciting journey - and somehow her experiences reflect that belief. Since both people live in the same world, the difference must come from their own thoughts. Often we are unaware of how much our beliefs shape our lives.

By uncovering limiting beliefs, we can understand why people behave as they do and help them to find more productive ways to view life. While this book explores communication between adults and children, you can apply the techniques to many other situations, including business and personal relationships.

THE LIMITS OF REWARDS AND WHAT REALLY MATTERS

A popular alternative to the "do it or else approach" is rewarding "good" behavior. Like adults, children enjoy games, toys, clothes, bikes, and novelties. Children's behavior can be directed so they can earn these objects. The catch comes with framing "learning as something one does in exchange for a prize rather than as something intrinsically valuable" to quote Alfie Kohn in *Punished by Rewards*. Like punishments, rewards can serve as a means to control children - and no one likes to be controlled by another.

As Madonna's song says, we live in a materialistic world, filled with materialistic boys and girls, who grow up into materialistic adults. There is no judgment being given here, just a statement of fact. But I do think that we can easily mislead children by overemphasizing the material and neglecting the inner world, where love, caring, and wisdom grow. Ken Keyes reminds us that "the true source of joy and happiness is inside ourselves."

I would like to share a story of how a strict rewards-based approach can affect people.

In the early eighties, I was teaching developmentally delayed (retarded) children. One endearing eight year old, Jeff, was finishing his swimming session. As he dried himself off, I knew the belabored ritual that would follow: a slow and distracted effort to dress himself. So I started to use the token economy I had established, rewarding him for certain behaviors.

"Hurry up and get dressed Jeff." Not looking up at me, he clumsily played with his towel.

"Jeff, if you dress right away I'll give you a token."

Jeff suddenly stopped jerking his towel and gazed up at me. "Then what will I get?"

"You will have one more token; so when you get enough, you can have a reward."

"Then what will I get?"

A wave of nervousness came over me. This wasn't a pet I was trying to train. I started to wonder if I was creating some sort of monster.

At that time, I couldn't articulate what was wrong, but I could feel that something was off. Despite my good intentions, I was out of alignment with another human being. I had lost touch, not knowing how this had happened.

Eventually I learned that there are ways to work with children other than control, life after rewards and punishments. Rewards have their place and use. We need to be careful, though, that we aren't sending the kid a message that the reason to act responsibly is to get an external reward. We connect with kids when we get inside their hearts and heads. Then they get the message that what they do does count. It doesn't require a big monetary investment, just some time to learn and be with children in a personal way. This book helps you find what's truly precious in kids - and how to nurture that so they value themselves.

TABLE 1
APPROACHES TO PROBLEM-SOLVING WITH CHILDREN

Method	Possible Results
• Authoritarian	Overdependence, rebellion, low self-esteem
• Rewards through Behavior Modification	External gratification, dependence on rewards, possible improvement often temporary
• Permissive	Lack of direction, irresponsibility, poor sense of boundaries
• 5 Steps	Positive internal beliefs, sense of responsibility, love, self-esteem

---

Table 1 summarizes different approaches to problem solving with children. Besides the two discussed in this chapter (Authoritarian and Rewards), I have included a Permissive approach and the 5-step approach I explore in this book.

While it's fine to spend money on kids, giving them the goodies they enjoy within reason, let's also build healthier relationships by giving them our attention and nurturing guidance. In the course of this book, you will learn specific ways to do that. You will learn methods that give you effective alternatives to being a rigid authoritarian or issuer of rewards.

CHAPTER TWO

Help Wanted:
Better Communicators

Many of the problems in our society reflect a breakdown in communication between adults and children. John Bradshaw observes that "the reason families get stuck and dysfunctional, even for generations, is because of their inability to cope with stress and come up with strategies that work."

The communication gap easily widens by the teen years. Traditionally, parents wield power over their children. Most of us were expected to obey orders blindly, without question. Not surprisingly, we did not say much in our defense. For generations, the belief has been reinforced that children are to be seen and not heard. It may have worked in the past, but it is becoming quite obvious that it is not working today.

THE OLD IS CRUMBLING

Think of how your parents dealt with you as a child when you had a problem or conflict.

- How much time did they spend with you?

- How confident and able were they to help you resolve difficulties?

- How were their listening skills?

- Did they demonstrate empathy when you spoke with them?

As a child, you probably wanted your parents to listen and understand what you were experiencing. Maybe that did not happen. And what about actually solving the problem?

- Was there a choice of different solutions for your problems?

- Who came up with the solutions?

- How much did you participate?

Most adults are unaware of a youngster's ability to problem solve, and as a result they habitually make decisions for the child.

The traditional authoritarian approach provides a clear-cut division of power. The adults have control; the children obey. When a problem exists, the adult swiftly provides a solution and the conversation is over. On the surface, this may seem an effective approach, but underneath it is a different story. The adult probably feels uncertain, wanting to help, but sensing something is missing. And as the child begins to mature, he or she feels resentful, wanting to be heard. Over time, it is easy to see how communication deteriorates, sometimes with disastrous results.

As a teacher, I have experienced my share of power struggles with students. It is uncomfortable and sets up conflicts in those around me and in myself. Outwardly, the adult puts on blinders, acting as if he knows what he's doing - frequently going into automatic - arbitrating, sometimes yelling and making a judgment with little or no input from the child, the one who is most affected by the decision.

What message does this authoritarian approach give to kids? They learn that they are incapable of solving problems for themselves. They also learn that you establish authority by rigid orders. By the teenage years, the search for independence can turn into intense rebellion. Youngsters want some power for themselves. If the childhood communication base is weak, it is easy to see why adolescents become so alienated.

Children need clear, safe boundaries for their development. The role of creating boundaries is part of the adult's responsibility. Boundaries need to be firm and consistent, carefully thought through for the child's welfare. The child's participation is also important in matters that directly concern the child. The adults must consider their own responsibility as well as the child's reasoning ability when setting boundaries. The more the child matures, the more the youngster can be involved with recognizing limits that are for his own welfare.

Our relationships with children have produced some disheartening results in the United States. The outcomes of these relationships litter the country, showing up in violence that includes a myriad of abuses. Here are a few telling statistics, some of them compiled by Roger Rosenblatt in his article "The Society that Pretends to Love Children." The findings are categorized under the headings of Child Abuse, Substance Abuse, and Violence and Crime. How many of these statistics relate to kids you know?

Statistics on Child Abuse:

- In 1993, according to interest groups, approximately three million children have been reported to public social service agencies for abuse or neglect. 1300 of those children died. (How many more cases went unreported?)

Statistics on Substance Abuse:

- A random sample of Minnesota adolescents found that six percent of middle to high income families had at least one child in alcohol or drug treatment programs by age 14 to 17. Findings also showed an additional five percent of adolescents using as many drugs and alcohol as those kids in treatment.

- A 1996 study found daughters to be 15 times likelier than their mothers to have begun using illegal drugs by age 15. The two year study, entitled "Substance Abuse and the American Woman," also found adolescent girls just as likely to have used alcohol and tobacco and illegal drugs as their male counterparts.

Statistics on Violence and Crime:

- A June 12, 1996, *USA Today* headline read "USA Almost Flunks Violence Report Card." The American Medical Association (AMA) gave the nation a "D" for violence for the second straight year The AMA's annual report card was based on statistical trends, public attitudes, treatment and prevention programs and costs of four categories of violence (family violence, sexual assault, public violence, and violence in entertainment).

- A 1996 comprehensive study by Rand Corporation found preventive programs are far more cost-effective in preventing crime over the long term than are mandatory sentences that imprison repeat adult offenders for extended periods. The report cited that investing in parent training programs could avert 157 crimes a year per state.

The essayist Mr. Rosenblatt offers a bleak overview of how we treat children. He writes that "one may go back through the 350 years [of American history] starting with the Puritans and discover an unbroken pattern of beating children, psychologically tormenting children, imposing one or another form of miseducation on them, forcing them into labor, giving them too little freedom, or too much."

In the past, it could be argued that parental domination helped the family stay together. That probably worked in simpler times, but our society is much more complex now.

As the problems children face change, we need to be willing to change too.

In today's world, adults repeatedly warn kids about the dangers of drugs, alcohol, sex and gangs... but to what effect? Lecturing kids and telling them to just say "no" to drugs and risky behavior is not enough. There are better ways to communicate and establish rapport with our children.

THE NEW IS EMERGING

It is remarkable that we've held together as well as we have. The growing trend of disobedience and violence among youngsters indicates a society in transition and transformation. Where is it heading? If we want children to listen, what do we as adults need to do?

Isn't the answer listening to the children so they will listen to us.

In the midst of the bad news about the American family, there are definitely signs of change in the air. Instead of the old "children are to be seen and not heard," you may have seen the billboard that reads: "A child is to be seen, not hurt." Society is waking up, beginning to provide ways for children to express themselves.

We know the sage advice: it's better to teach someone how to fish than simply to give them a fish. With kids, it's better to involve them with problem solving than to give the solution to them. And, of course, we can provide the necessary boundaries, so the solutions satisfy both you and the child.

When kids do participate in solving problems, their self-esteem grows. In contrast, being shut out of that process makes them feel helpless and resentful. When babies are born, they depend on their parents to provide for their needs. Yet even their cries and responses demonstrate the beginnings of interaction in the problem solving process.

By the time they enter kindergarten, kids have begun to solve some of their own problems. In grade school they have the intellect and cognitive skills to participate in increasingly complex problems that arise as they interact with others.

Many parents, however, still respond to them in the same way they did to the newborn. This stifles the child's preparation for going out into the world, where they must handle life's challenges.

How then can the child make the transitions? As the child grows, so too should his or her involvement in solving problems.

CONFLICT RESOLUTION

The term conflict resolution refers to creating solutions by having the participants brainstorm different possibilities. The goal is to generate many possible answers from which to choose. But a possible pitfall exists: if the people generating the answers are an adult and a child, guess who will probably dominate the process? Conflict resolution can be biased toward adult control and decision-making. Addressing this possible imbalance, *Getting Thru to Kids* explores different ways to find solutions.

Another limitation of conflict resolution is it does not attend to the cause of the problem. So even though good solutions may be found, the problem may recur since the original source that produced the trouble remains.

In the 5-step problem solving method found in this book, the child finds solutions with the adult's guidance and input when needed. The child is empowered by discovering answers to his own problem, which includes transforming what caused the problem in the first place. The kid finds new beliefs, broadening his outlook. The adult becomes a key supporter and facilitator in the process.

From my experience, this approach represents a big change for most adults. To simplify it, I have developed a 5-step process, which is the essence of this book. With the 5 Steps, the adult listens to the child's problem and the child's associated feelings, thoughts, and limiting beliefs. Then, after defining the boundaries, the adult guides the child to find a more productive, harmonious belief.

As a result, a new picture of the situation emerges. The original troubled image dissolves... and an uplifting vision of the future replaces it. When the process is complete, both parties have had the opportunity to express themselves and come up with an acceptable resolution.

Your path is becoming clear. You can step out of the old limitations that accompanied your growing up. Then take a look around at the current alarming trends of abuse and violence. You can move in another direction. You can choose to consciously work with kids. And that makes all the difference in the world.

CHAPTER THREE

The Five Steps to Breakthrough Communication

You know what it's like when your communication does not work. To give an example, let me briefly describe a family situation and how a parent tries to resolve it. It is not too harmonious but quite common.

Eight year old Vincent wants to play with his older sister's Game Gear, the handheld portable video game system. Fourteen year old Jazz doesn't want to be bothered by her younger brother. She concentrates on the Game Gear challenge, speeding her animated motorcycle along the bumpy road with all its obstacles.

The motorcycle swerves into another cycle, and a police car pulls her over.

But something more disturbing pesters her. Vincent, having strategically seated himself on the sofa a few feet away from his sister and the game, keeps asking when he can play the hypnotic game.

After a few inquiries that his sister ignores, Vincent asks Jazz, "Are you going to play that game forever?"

"No," his sister curtly answers, still focusing on her colorful cycle as it turns the corner, heading toward another bump in the road.

Becoming desperate, Vincent tries to grab the game from her. Jazz swiftly avoids the foray by elbowing his hand away from the game, still keeping her eyes fixed on the game's roadway. Vincent leaves, kicking the garbage can on his way out of the room.

The phone rings and Jazz rushes out to answer, leaving the Game Gear behind on the couch. Peering out from down the hallway, Vincent sees his chance. He returns to his sister's room and seizes his desire while sis talks on the kitchen phone.

Later that day, Jazz asks her mother how her Game Gear had been moved. She wonders if mom saw Vincent playing with it. "Come to think of it, I have seen him playing with it," mom responds.

Vincent enters the room and turns on the TV, plopping himself down in the overstuffed armchair. Jazz rushes over to him.

"Have you played with my Game Gear? It's not where I left it."

"No, I haven't seen it."

"You're lying!"

"No, I'm not." Vincent continues to watch the television as his sister storms out of the room. The mother goes over to handle the situation.

Mom turns off the TV, puts her hands on her hips and looks down at Vincent seated in the armchair. "Vincent, I saw you take your sister's Game Gear. What do you think you're doing? You keep doing this again and again. I'm tired of this lying. This has got to stop. You're in trouble now. You're not going to watch TV for a week! I'm so frustrated from your behavior; I don't know what I'm going to do."

Let's pause this scene. It's kind of ugly isn't it? Yet I have played the frustrated adult role myself, feeling helpless and out of control as the kid continues the same patterns of misbehavior. It feels as though the child shields himself behind a brick wall as you hurl paper wads.

Let's replay the last scene from the time the mom enters. This time she will take a different approach to her son. She again turns off the TV. But instead of looking down at him and lecturing, she calmly goes over to the couch next to Vincent and sits in a comfortable position similar to the way he sits.

"Vincent, why did you take your sister's Game Gear without permission?"

"I didn't take it."

The mother calmly responds, "I saw you using it. Now why didn't you tell me the truth?"

"I thought I'd get in trouble."

"So what will lying do?"

"It gets me out of trouble."

"You believe lying gets you out of trouble. How do you feel when you lie?"

"Bad."

"You feel kind of sad, maybe ashamed of what you did?"

"Uh huh."

"It doesn't sound as if you like feeling that way. Let's see: did it get you out of trouble?"

"No."

"Did you hurt anyone by lying? Like me or your sister or yourself?"

"Yes."

"So what can you say about this situation?"

"I'll tell the truth."

"That's a good way of looking at it. So next time you have trouble, say with a poor report card, what will you do?"

"Tell the truth."

"Good. Now you know there are consequences for what you did to your sister?"

"Yes. Not play with her Game Gear for a week?"

"Sounds like a reasonable consequence. Let's see what she says."

The replayed scene was far different from the first tirade the mom gave to her son. The second time mom listened. She was patient and calm despite her disappointment with Vincent. She let Vincent share his feelings and thoughts. They worked together to arrive at a new approach, telling the truth, which the son volunteered to try. Vincent had a chance to take responsibility for himself and come to new realizations. A deep communication took place.

DEEP COMMUNICATION AND PROBLEM SOLVING, AN OVERVIEW

To develop deeper communication with a child, I have mapped out the process into 5 Steps:

1. **Problem:** Identify the child's problem.

2. **Feelings:** Find out what the child is feeling about the problem

3. **Off belief:** Have the child discover the underlying belief - thought process - that causes the awkwardness and problem.

4. **On belief:** Through examination and reasoning, allow the child to find a better, more enhancing belief.

5. **Future Vision:** Let the child envision the future with the new belief installed.

To provide a general idea of the process, I want to show you an example of how a problem can be transformed by the 5 Steps.

- **Step One is identifying the *problem*.** What is bothering the person? Twelve year old Stephanie is disturbed by another girl bragging around her. That is her problem. The adult who is helping Stephanie identifies this difficulty as the first step in the process.

- **Step Two is finding the *feelings* about the situation.** Through questioning, the adult finds out that Stephanie feels hurt and angry around the bragging child. The situation triggers feelings the girl has about herself and her relationship to others.

- **Step Three reveals the** *off belief*. This is what the girl believes about herself and the situation. Probing deeper, the adult finds that Stephanie's thoughts form a restrictive pattern, a limiting belief about how to view the world. Beneath her feelings of hurt and anger, Stephanie believes that she is a victim, helpless and out of control. She says, "I can't handle this situation and the other girl makes me angry."

- **Step Four shifts to an** *on belief*. This is where the change happens. The adult helps the child change the limiting belief to one that is opening, enhancing and liberating. In this case, Stephanie discovers that she can shift her belief from "I can't handle it" to "I can handle it." A simple "can" makes all the difference.

- **Step Five in the process concerns the** *future vision*. With adult help, Stephanie can see, hear and feel the future differently after installing the new belief. She imagines herself calmly seated around the bragging child, breathing slowly, body relaxed. Instead of considering herself a victim, she now sees herself being comfortable and in control of herself.

Table 3 is a simple example of a problem that may seem small to an adult, but may be torture to a child. Now that you have a brief overview of the 5 Steps let's examine each part more closely.

TABLE 3
BELIEFS, FEELINGS AND OUTCOMES

Stephanie's *Off* Belief	Negative Feelings	Negative Outcome
I can't *handle the* *situation*	*hurt* *angry* *afraid*	*Stephanie is* *disturbed by* *the bragging girl*
Stephanie's *On* Belief	Positive Feelings	Positive Outcome
I can *handle the* *situation*	*confident* *calm* *optimistic*	*Stephanie is* *comfortable around* *the bragging girl*

Notice how the problem and solution start off with the belief. In turn, the belief generates feelings that create experiences. The 5 Steps show the underlying cause of the problem, the restrictive belief. The new belief and solution can have lasting results since it transforms the source of the trouble.

CHAPTER FOUR

Problem Solving Step-by-Step

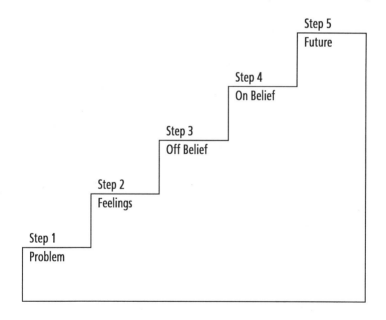

This chapter examines each step, providing the specifics to communicate more effectively.

☐ STEP 1: IDENTIFYING THE PROBLEM

This first step of the process - identifying the problem - is probably familiar to adults. Adults often already have the wisdom to do this step and just need to be calm enough themselves to ask the child what happened and listen to the kid's explanation.

Even though this first step may be obvious, it can be omitted or distorted. We sometimes assume what is wrong with the child before he has even had a chance to tell us. We may jump to conclusions or mistakenly associate this situation with another.

Taking time to have the child explain the problem is crucial. When you listen carefully to the child, he will feel free to express himself. Listening shows respect and helps attend to the problem. Listening also creates an environment of trust to solve problems and heal wounds.

An important note: A key to starting the process is determining whether the child is actually ready to speak about the problem. Timing is important and the kid needs to be willing to share the trouble he experiences. Pushing the child to speak will alienate him and increase the reluctance to talk. If he is in denial about the problem or too disturbed, wait until the time is right - which may take minutes or days. Your patience and respect for the child will greatly enhance your efforts.

☐ STEP 2: EXPRESSING FEELINGS

Our male-dominated culture tends to discount feelings. This has to do with a masculine view, of being a "man" and taking it, that is, not showing feelings. Feelings are for sissies, wimps or girls. As one forty year old basketball player harshly remarked after a teammate missed a few shots, "You're going to have to start wearing a skirt." Translation: feelings are feminine and considered a weakness.

How does this "feel-less" cultural attitude translate to childrearing? Feelings tend to be downplayed or dismissed, especially by males. Males can be angry; females can cry. But that's pretty much the limit. If males cry, they're too feminine; if females get angry, they're too masculine.

When we avoid feelings, they do not disappear - they simply go into hiding.

Emotions are buried in our subconscious and stored in our bodies. They carry powerful energy that can be unleashed or directed.

It is a matter of recognizing and guiding the energy, or feelings will come out haphazardly, putting us at their mercy.

It is tempting to just tell the child what he feels. But for the child to benefit, let him describe his own feelings. The child then increases his awareness and you grow more in touch with him, creating empathy by careful listening. As he safely expresses uncomfortable feelings, the child feels nurtured and supported. The child does most of the talking but appreciates the adult's silent supportive presence.

When he is at a loss then you can help him with wording. Just be sure that you are not preventing the child from adequately expressing himself by cutting him off or putting words into his mouth. Allow time for the process, so the kid can examine himself and discover his feelings. On occasion you might disclose having those feelings yourself. Be in the moment, guided by your heart and the situation.

At times the youngster may need help to find words that fit feelings. Just saying one is feeling "good," "fine," "bad," "nothing," or "okay" is not descriptive of feelings. Help the child with words such as "excited," "happy," "sad," "lonely," "frustrated," and "confused" to describe feelings.

If you help the child with the words be sure he agrees with the wording. If possible, use the words the child says.

You are not trying to convince the child about what you're saying; rather you are trying to help define the child's experience and feelings.

Realize that a problem triggers multiple feelings. Take your time to recognize and sort them out. Often you will find they come down to feeling fear. Fear thrives in an absence of knowledge and love. To bridge this gap, the subsequent steps of the process help the person develop understanding and self-esteem.

If you are around the child regularly, also note if there is a tendency for him to always describe the same feeling. This may signal that the child is hiding another feeling that he feels is unacceptable to have. The youngster may have received a message that certain feelings are wrong to express. The child then conceals certain feelings because they have made his caretakers uncomfortable. He then covers up the unacceptable feeling with another more acceptable one. For example, the child may consider it okay to have sadness but not anger. Or to have anger but not fear.

BREATHE THROUGH THE FEELINGS

When tension arises for you or the child be aware of the breathing pattern. Negative feelings tend to constrict our breathing, getting caught in the throat and chest. Holding back and stuffing emotions interferes with our energy flow. *Deep aware breathing helps us release emotions and clear blockages.* While experiencing feelings, practice taking deep breaths, releasing on the exhales.

Daniel Goleman's book *Emotional Intelligence: Why It Can Matter More than IQ* elaborates on how feelings are a critical yet overlooked part of our growth. He writes, "I can foresee a day when education will routinely include inculcating essential human competencies such as self-awareness, self-control, and empathy, and the arts of listening, resolving conflicts, and cooperation." He goes on to explore how "emotional literacy" can civilize our society and protect us from the ravages of violence.

Learning which feelings exist and how to distinguish them takes time. But it's an investment that will yield results over a lifetime. You can find an aid to identifying feelings in Appendix B.

It will help your communication if you practice identifying feelings, which are occurring virtually all the time. To identify your feelings, complete the sentence, "I feel...." Try it on yourself now. And use it with a child at your first opportunity.

When expressing feelings, you want to avoid blaming another person for your own feelings. The feelings belong to the person who expresses them. Taking ownership of feelings empowers people of all ages. Blaming another for one's feelings disempowers, saying another person controls you.

Note when you associate someone else's behavior as a trigger for your own feelings. The next step is to sort out your feelings from the other person's actions. You can claim your own feelings by being descriptive with the word "I" rather than using the accusatory word "you." For example, "I feel irritated when you leave your cards all over the table," instead of "You irritate me when you're a slob." A child might say, "I get mad when you yell," rather than "You're a stupid loudmouth."

Using these "I feel sentences" can be a powerful way to express yourself. It is a healthy habit to develop for adults and children.

STEP 3: FINDING THE OFF BELIEF

Underlying our feelings are beliefs. It is beliefs that give rise to feelings. They also create attitudes, decisions, and choices. Beliefs have far-reaching affects and hold a powerful influence on our life.

In beliefs, you find the source of the problem. This will lead to its solution and the possibility of newfound beliefs.

When you recognize and change beliefs you go beyond altering behavior. A person's whole outlook changes. This explains why the approach of simply changing a child's behavior can have little impact on his internal world and self-esteem. For example, let's take a child who believes things are unfair. After your discussion about his sportsmanship, he may agree to change his behavior about not yelling when he disagrees with an umpire's call during a softball game. But his outlook stays unchanged. He remains ever ready to create other behaviors to reflect this belief about an unfair world (such as complaining to his teammates).

Epictetus, the ancient Roman philosopher, noted it is not events themselves but how we view them that affect us. We filter the world through what we believe. For example, the person who sees the world as a cruel place frequently feels anxious and scared. Whereas a person who views the world as a friendly place feels calm, adventurous, and confident. Naturally particular situations and environments influence the way beliefs play themselves out.

Where do beliefs originate? In early childhood, beliefs form from our experiences, our needs and how parents treat us. Initially, the child wants love and approval from his family. As the child grows, peer influence comes into play. Although beliefs may change, they still continue to frame how the child views the world.

How do you tell when beliefs limit and distort? Off beliefs say you are better than or worse than others. This outlook causes you to separate from others, feeling inadequate, defective, and flawed. As a result of being cut off from yourself and others, you feel helpless and victimized. You then continually seek to prove your restrictive belief and create self-fulfilling prophecies about yourself and the world. Not surprisingly, many troubles stem from such a blocked vantage point because if you look for trouble, you will probably find it.

You can discover beliefs by examining thought patterns. To find an off belief, review an area of difficulty in your life or a child's life. What are the feelings about it? When difficult feelings arise, remember to keep breathing deeply. Now notice the thoughts around the problem. What pattern or generalization is present? Therein lies an inhibiting belief.

Do things seem out of control? Are people viewed as adversaries? Are there thoughts of hopelessness and despair of trying? Such beliefs undermine even many valiant efforts to change. Limiting beliefs polarize, pitting one person against another, placing the person at odds with himself and others. Whether he sees himself as more than or less than others, the person ends up judging himself as inadequate. Off beliefs connect to judgments that devalue yourself and others. For

---

TABLE 4:
HOW BELIEFS CREATE BELIEF SYSTEMS

Off Beliefs	On Beliefs
"Life is unfair."	"Things work out."
"No one likes me."	"I am included."
"I can't do this work."	"I can improve."
create	create
Restrictive Belief System	Productive Belief System
"I don't care."	"Life is an adventure."

---

further information on specific kinds of beliefs see Appendices C and D.

A collection of beliefs forms a belief system. For example, limiting beliefs such as "life is unfair," "I don't get what I want" and "nobody likes me" form a belief system of "it doesn't matter." This creates what is commonly called a "bad" attitude such as "I don't care about anything." Similarly, enhancing beliefs like "life is fair" and "I feel included" form an uplifting belief system like "life is an adventure." This in turn creates a productive attitude, which fosters caring and compassion. By transforming individual off beliefs to on beliefs eventually entire belief systems shift. Frowns turn into smiles. (Table 4 summarizes this process.)

It is helpful to recognize and accept that we all have our off and on beliefs. Be compassionate and patient with yourself

---

DEMANDS

Demands come from impatience, aggressively trying to control the situation.

Demands serve inhibiting beliefs with their "shoulds," "musts," and "I have tos." Check for tone of voice: demands rise out of frustration; more positive beliefs repose in calm, confident tones.

Teaching social skills shows the child how to transform demands into requests. For example, you can demonstrate how to use appropriate language and tone of voice. Requests are a far more suitable form of communication than demands.

and others, knowing you are making significant efforts. You are paving the way for yourself and others.

STEP 4: SHIFTING TO THE ON BELIEF

So now that the limiting belief has surfaced what next? It's time to play "Truth," "Consequences" or "Change." These three approaches reveal the off belief as a distortion... leading the person to naturally seek a more positive outlook. The child, then, naturally changes his or her position - going from an off believer to an on believer.

a)   Shifting from Off to On Belief Playing "Truth"

To play "Truth" investigate a belief that uses absolutes like "always," "never," "everyone," and "nobody." Discover the truth behind such beliefs as "I *never* get what I want"; "*No one* likes me"; "Life is *always* unfair." By finding exceptions to these thought patterns, a new understanding emerges. Beliefs shift to "*Sometimes* I get what I want"; "*Some* people like me"; and "Life *can* be fair." In this way life becomes more acceptable, empowering the person to deal with a spectrum of possibilities.

Remember these tips to dismantle negative beliefs when you play "Truth":

• *Question absolutist beliefs* by asking, "Have you ever... [received what you want, had someone like you, been treated fairly]?"

- *Use qualifying phrases* to eliminate generalizations. Find terms like "often," "sometimes," "it seems that."

- Note down other generalizations from the 5 Steps and your daily experience.

b) Shifting from Off to On Belief Playing "Consequences"

To play "Consequences," just calmly think through the results of using the belief in question. Keep exploring how the restrictive viewpoint affects what does or could happen. In other words, what are the consequences of the off belief?

Using "Consequences" works well when the belief leads to failure. Insisting on perfection is a common way people set themselves up for a fall. For instance, take a belief like "I can't make a mistake." If one believes perfection is a necessity, what will result? Anxious, angry irritable feelings... volatile temper... overcompetitiveness... aggression... belittling of others... to name a few. This will clearly be undesirable to children and adults alike. So the new belief may be something like "I can learn from my mistakes."

You can also play "Consequences" with a belief about school like "I can't do this work." (For example, the work is "stupid" as people sometimes say.) What are the results of such a belief? One will give up easily. The person might set unrealistic expectations. Cheating might come into play. A lot of frustration and anger will be experienced. Believing "I can't do school work" posts a red flag for failure.

But this can be turned around. With some self-examination and appropriate questions, the person will naturally seek a better belief about schoolwork, such as "I can try" or "I can improve." The process works when the person

RELEASING ANGER

It has been said that rage and anger can destroy one's heritage. Dealing with anger is sometimes as volatile a process as the emotion itself. Still, anger can be cleanly processed, rationally discussed and connected to underlying beliefs.

Anger allows you to say no, to establish safe boundaries preventing abusive relationships. Identifying feelings grounds you in your body instead of spacing out and denying what you are experiencing. Explore the underlying emotions - such as hurt and fear - that fuel the anger. As you connect with anger, you get in touch with yourself, your inner truth and conscience.

Sometimes children, particularly males, say that destructive behavior releases their tensions when angry. In these cases, the child may be taking on another person's anger. A guideline is to return the unwanted anger back to the owner and keep your own. This can be done by visualizing or speaking to the person who sent the anger to you in the first place. If speaking to another, be sure that it is safe and that you are not putting yourself at risk.

If the child says he wants to be violent, you can acknowledge the child for this admission, then ask him about the consequences of violent behavior. By exploring the negative effects of such behavior, the child sees the downside, opening himself to alternative actions. Discuss the long-term consequences of angry destruction, including such tolls as ruined trust, property, and possible physical harm.

Educate the child that acknowledging anger can release it. It can also reveal undermining beliefs. Stuffing anger bottles the energy inside the body, imploding on organs and exploding in destructive behavior. Besides openly discussing emotions, anger can be released safely by participating in sports or arts. Movement channels the energy in constructive ways.

comes to this realization herself, not because someone told or convinced her. As a result, the person's will and determination develop.

Here are some helpful phrases for *eliminating "catastrophizing,"* seeing the world as a disastrous place filled with failure. Examples are in brackets:

- "I don't like... [it when people criticize me]."

- "It might be embarrassing, but I'll survive... [if I don't get that outfit]."

- "I can handle it... [if I make a mistake]."

The right words will present themselves as you naturally follow the process. The negative consequences of the off belief will motivate the person to seek a better way, finding positive consequences.

c) Shifting from Off to On Belief by Playing "Change"

The third way to shift from a negative to positive belief involves "Change." Using the other approaches - "Truth" or "Consequences" - can take longer, involving more questions that challenge the nature of the off belief. The third approach - "Change" - has the person simply wanting to immediately change the unproductive belief. There may be a certain "ah ha" of realization. Got a bad belief? Why not get a better one.

So if the belief says "Things are unfair," then ask what would make it fair or fairer?

If the first response is "nothing," just patiently stay with it. Realize that children, like adults, are quite resourceful, more than we might initially think. If the child thinks her grade was unfair, a number of possibilities may emerge: go talk with the teacher, study harder, pay more attention, see what can be learned from the situation or just accept it. All of these strategies will make "it fairer," - the world opens up with possibilities, despair and hopelessness fall away.

How could you and the child play "Change" with the belief "I am left out"? The way to "Change" being left out - the remedy - is to become more included. Start to generate ways to be included. Talk to people about the problem. Study those who are popular as role models. Find ways to like yourself more. Remember what you did when you were included. Find others with common interests. Develop new interests for yourself that can attract others to you.

In playing "Change" for new beliefs help the kid start developing a *language of taking responsibility*. Help the young person understand he can change, which will give him a sense of power and responsibility.

Use phrases like (examples are again in brackets):

- "I am responsible for... [my own feelings]."

- "It's up to me to... [get my work done]."

- "I'm the one who will need to... [be more flexible]."

- "Nobody else is responsible for... [cleaning my room or body]."

As a further guideline, positive beliefs grow when we *state our preferences*. Use phrases like:

- "I prefer... [keeping things the way they are, but I can deal with change]."

- "I want... [that bike but I can live without it]."

- "It's okay if... [I have to ask before touching other's belongings]."

This kind of moderate language establishes flexibility and well-being, qualities of enhancing beliefs.

Use the previous information to help you choose which approach to use in opening up beliefs. Each way - "Truth," "Consequences" or "Change" - can powerfully transform an off belief to an on belief. By practicing and being in the moment, your intuitive sense will lead you which way to go.

Beliefs come down to a few simple words. But those select words hold a vast power that can imprison us or liberate us.

Change a few words and your life can profoundly change. Awareness is the key that opens the door.

How can you discern when beliefs are life-affirming? First check your feelings and thoughts to see whether they are coming from fear or love. You can also notice the reflections of your thinking in the situations that you attract in your life. Enhancing beliefs honor and develop your uniqueness and others. They foster security, caring, trust, and respect - positive beliefs open the door to wholeness.

By helping kids find on beliefs, you guide them to love themselves and others. And that kind of help is a loving act in itself.

STRATEGIES TO FOLLOW UP NEW BELIEFS

Strategies naturally emerge from on beliefs. For instance, say the child comes to a new understanding that "Some people like me." Then she may start planning ways to spend time with those people. Also, the final part of the 5 Steps, Future Vision, will fortify her new belief.

You may want to help the child find additional ways to actualize the newfound belief. If the child now believes she can handle criticism, she can journal on her thoughts and feelings, do artwork, compose a scrapbook or montage. Any way to focus and reinforce the new belief.

Another excellent strategy is to role play with the child. Take the role of the critic and see how the child responds. Reverse roles, you play the child and she criticizes you. This gives her practical ideas on how to deal with criticism and integrate new understandings.

The goal is to create heart-centered beliefs that affirm the person's life and potential. By developing such an outlook, positive boundaries are put in place.

Remember it may take time to strengthen and integrate the new belief. The old belief may still be there, but over time the child can rely on the new belief. There are many suggestions throughout this book on how to reinforce the child's new outlook.

More elaborate self-discovery processes often need trained guidance and are outside the scope of this work. See the bibliography for the Winkleman and Stone books if you want to research further.

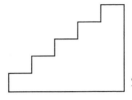

STEP 5: CREATING THE FUTURE

Let's review how far you have come. First you have identified the problem. Next you found the feelings associated with that difficulty. Underlying the feelings stirred thought patterns, solidifying into a restrictive belief. Then through reasoning and strategies - such as "Truth, "Consequences" or "Change" - a positive belief was discovered.

After exploring the thoughts and feelings of the first four steps, a person experiences a change. The problem recedes as a new expression and receptivity develop. A successful process lets you favorably see a future that used to be viewed as unwelcome.

The final step of the process comes with envisioning a positive future, what NLP calls future pace. This future vision uses the senses to get a fuller picture of the future. By imagining sight, sound, feelings, and sometimes taste and smell, you can powerfully realize the future.

Let's say Maria has a newfound belief about schoolwork: "I can improve." Previously she would look at her books with distaste, tap her hand nervously and try to avoid the work. Now with a new positive outlook, what would her future vision be, a vision reflecting an "I can improve" attitude? ...She sees herself staying with her schoolbook (sight), hears her calm breathing (sound) and feels relaxed in the body (sensation). As she studies, she also takes a sip from her water glass (taste).

To further enhance the vision, you can add a color. Just ask the kid to associate a color with the new scene. Whatever color she chooses is the right one.

A note: For some adults, the idea of using a color in problem solving seems strange or foreign. But remember that children enjoy visualizing colors, just like painting with different hues. It opens up a person's creativity and imagination. Imagine what color this information evokes for you right now. Whatever you see or sense is the right color. If you want to change it, feel free to do so. I think you will find children of all ages - from one to a hundred - enjoy the color spectrum, and it can resolve problems in a fun and effective way.

To further familiarize you with the future vision process, let's take one more example. Jason's new on belief is "I can handle people criticizing me" (before he believed that he couldn't handle it). So what would his future vision be? ...Jason sees himself on the softball field looking composed when a teammate criticizes him (sight and sound). He breathes calmly and relaxes his shoulders (body sensations). His color for this new vision is blue, which he sees in the sky as it tints the whole scene. He takes in the scent of the nearby fir trees (smell).

The future vision deepens the problem solving resolution. By checking the kid's new picture, you determine how convinced the person really is about his new outlook. Is the future vision clear? Is it desirable and rejuvenating?

If the new future is dim, you may want to find out which sense - sight, sound, feeling - the child relates to most easily in order to strengthen the vision. If the person cannot see the future, find out his vision through an alternative sense. Instead of seeing, the kid could sense what his body would feel like during a positive future. Or to use his other sense, the kid could find out what sounds - words, voices, nature sounds - he hears in the successful upcoming situation.

If he draws a blank, acknowledge that he is experiencing some difficulty. Then help him focus by asking him to use his imagination. Use the prompting words "what if." "*What if* you could hear the sounds, or see the picture or feel the sensations?" The idea is to encourage the child and build confidence in his own new future vision.

You can also play with the different aspects of future visioning. Here are examples.

For *sight*:

- Make the picture brighter, change the colors, bring the screen closer or make it bigger.

For *sounds*:

- Change the volume or pitch.

For *feelings and sensations*:

- Intensify them or spread them over more of the body.

Tastes and *smells* can be sharpened also.

Returning to our earlier example, if Maria can't hear any sounds when she envisions herself studying, then she can focus on the picture. Make the picture of Maria concentrating with her book larger and brighter. Intensify the color she associates with the scene. By using her visualizing abilities, Maria will feel more competent as she completes the 5 Steps.

Or, if Jason is having difficulty seeing himself on the softball field, have him focus on his breathing to put himself at ease. Or have him spend time relaxing parts of his body. If he is slow to picture the vision, then turn to body sensations or sounds to realize his future. Build on the person's strengths, the senses that are most developed.

If you process through a problem and the future still seems bleak, there may be more exploring to do. Here are possible directions to take if the future vision is shaky:

- Perhaps the child with the problem is still doubtful of the new on belief. It may require reexamining the positive belief to be sure it is acceptable and worded correctly.

- Maybe more time is needed to integrate the learning.

- There may be other associated problems, which can be addressed through the 5 Steps or an alternative approach.

As we know, the mind is very powerful. Our images of reality greatly influence how we experience the world. When we have a problem, we see this area as troubled with accompanying sights, sounds, and feelings. And when we have an agreeable view, our senses correspond with uplifting images.

The future vision caps the problem solving process, insuring greater success after the child finishes the 5 Steps.

IMPLEMENTING THE 5 STEPS

Take a moment to see if you have the five steps memorized. Familiarizing yourself with the 5 Steps can be likened to an actress learning her lines. Once memorizing the words, the actress concentrates more on what her part actually means. So like a skillful actress, just knowing the names of the 5 Steps

---

HOLOGRAMS

The mind has been described as a hologram, where every part contains the whole. This means that any particular portion of your problem represents the entire problem with all its ugliness and disharmony. When you go through the 5 Steps your hologram shifts. Each aspect of the former problem can turn harmonious, with the colors, shapes, sounds, sensations and feelings you enjoy. So even partial success with the problem solving process can shift your reality, transforming the whole. It is like improving a painting, as you add each color and shade the whole picture grows more attractive. As your hologram grows in harmony, so too does your communication.

---

allows you to focus more on your dialogue and communication flow. Then there is the actual flow of doing the 5 Steps. Here are two helpful tips:

- If you get stuck along the way, you can work with the belief "it takes time to learn" and then move on.

- As a memory aid, you can use a cue card with the 5 Steps listed on it. You can carry this cue card with you while learning the process.

The 5 Steps lead you from a problem, to feelings, to negative beliefs, to positive beliefs, to a new future vision. It's quite a journey. The process naturally evolves and may go at varying speeds, with bumps along the way. Just stay with it as each thought and feeling come up. If you don't know what to do or say, just *allow* the answer to emerge. This may take periods of silence to let deeper understanding and answers bubble up to consciousness.

I know many times I have become stuck in the process. I just remember to allow myself time, sometimes sweating through nervous pauses and confusion. I know there is sunlight behind the clouds. The answer will come. Though pauses sometimes seem to last forever, I have accustomed myself to not knowing the answer and having to be right. I have been wrong too many times. Let the process do its work.

Be neutral and open, trust the process. Even if it does not totally work out, much can be learned. It's not about getting it right; it's about being there so the communication can flow the way it wants. The 5 Steps are guideposts along the way.

After you process with a kid, he probably will be proud of all he has accomplished for himself and how much you have listened to him. The person you have helped has gone from experiencing a gloomy problem to discovering a new belief, leading to a brighter future.

Give yourself permission to feel good about what you accomplished with the communication, how you helped yourself and others. You have traded in arguing and proving yourself "right." In return you are free to let go and be yourself, a human being who expresses himself more fully and allows others to do the same.

CHAPTER FIVE

Your Role in Getting *thru* to Kids

So now you are getting a sense of the 5 Steps, having some information and a few trials and errors under your belt. A picture is developing of adult-child communication. Yet you may wonder about how to fit into this new role, this different way of communicating. Here are some further guidelines and skills to secure your footing through the process.

KEEPING YOUR SELF-CONTROL

A prerequisite to doing the 5 Steps calls for you to be calm enough yourself to talk with the youngster. How can you get the kid to open up if you are distraught and impatient? Now this does not mean you have to be totally calm before processing. Sometimes that is impractical and unrealistic.

Certainly being a saint isn't a requirement to process with a child. Yet a certain degree of self-control is necessary for adults to get through to kids. By showing self-composure you are role modeling. As you find the appropriate words and tone of voice to use, you are helping the child immeasurably, teaching by example. It is fine to indicate a degree of irritation with the child if you are forthright and attentive to the child's responses. By being in the moment, you will have a sense of how to proceed.

If the situation upsets you, consider looking at your own limiting beliefs. Adults have their own set of restrictive beliefs and they can be easily passed on to children. To help you get a handle on your own interfering thought processes, consider using the 5 Steps on yourself (see Appendix F).

An added benefit: both you and the child often experience a calming influence by using the process itself.

AVOIDING POWER STRUGGLES AND LECTURING

Power struggles with children are ineffective and quickly drain your energy. If you keep repeating your words, raising your voice and experiencing frustration, you may have engaged in a battle with the kid you are trying to help. Remember, in the 5 Steps you are aiming to help the child problem solve. Being serviceable to the youngster is the key. If the child's issues affect you directly then share those concerns (see Chapter Six on "Expressing Your Needs and Concerns" for more information).

You can detect power struggles by the words you use with the child. Take this example: the child says, "I never get what I want [off belief]." Then you respond, "I never get you what you want?" This response may be the trigger for a battle to begin.

Here is a "bullet to bullet" analysis of this power struggle, followed by a summary table:

- Your reply - "I never get you what you want?" - can come across as trying to "convince" the child. You may feel indignant that the youngster doesn't appreciate your previous efforts to help the child.

- It is fine for you to feel frustrated with the child, but trying to convince the child that he is wrong leads to arguments and resistance.

- Instead, you can straightforwardly ask the kid, "Have you ever gotten what you wanted?" Notice that the emphasis is on the child ("you"), not the adult.

- Now contrast this new response - "Have you ever gotten what you wanted?" - with your original response of "I never get what you want."

- The words are similar but the meaning is quite different.

- The first response - "I never get you what you want?" - challenges and provokes the child. Remember that the child has just stated the off belief of never getting what he wants. So the kid wonders why you repeat the belief back to him in a way that implies disagreement without openly saying so.

- You may want to point out the error in the child's all or nothing thinking. However, the first response - "I never get you what you want?" - can come across as irritating and argumentative to the kid.

- The alternative response - "Have you ever gotten what you wanted?" - gives the youngster a chance to think about the situation. By his own awareness he can realize the error in his belief system. This second way of questioning the off belief invites self-examination by the child and allows you to facilitate (not manipulate) the answers.

- Refer to Table 5.1 for a summary of these responses.

Power struggles also arise when you lecture kids. One-sided "discussions" tend to be overbearing and longwinded. Children feel talked at and talked down to. A prolonged scolding oppresses others and can become verbally abusive. Children become disempowered, feeling shamed, rebellious, and passive-aggressive.

Lecturing tends to reinforce negative beliefs.

Lectures harden judgment and hatred about ourselves and others. Beneath these condemnations lie opinions that we are flawed. Lecturing just heightens that sense of inadequacy.

YOUR OWN PROCESSING

Besides being calm and avoiding power struggles, another aspect of processing has to do with ownership of problems. If *you* are upset, consider that the problem:

- Can belong to you rather than the child.
- Can belong to both you and child.

TABLE 5.1
COMPARISON OF ADULT'S RESPONSES

Adult's Ineffective Response	vs.	Adult's Effective Response:
"I never get you what you want?"		*"Have you ever gotten what you wanted?"*
adult indirect, maybe manipulative		adult open and neutral
Negative Results		**Positive Results**
adult trying to convince child		child considers for himself
can invite child to resist, argue		invites child to self-examine
can oppose the child's belief		child thinks through beliefs
creates power struggle		adult works with child

It is healthy for you to take ownership of your own problems, especially in light of asking children to take responsibility for their problems. *Getting Thru* improves by practicing the process on yourself, possibly on an ongoing basis. And don't worry, you will find plenty of material. As long as problems exist, you have something to process and learn.

What if you are afraid to look at your problems? Most likely those problems are already interfering with your life, including areas concerning children. You may need to ask yourself, "What needs to be done to put *my own* house in order?"

The 5 Steps is one of many resources. You can also find help for yourself from books and tapes, friends, advisors, counselors, therapists and family, wherever you feel drawn to go. A problem already exists and now you are admirably seeking to remedy it. By growing and moving on with your life, you can help yourself and others.

What if you are not sure where to find a problem? Look for any discomfort you experience. Any feeling that has a "charge" on it, causing unease, signals that a blockage exists. This problem waits for a solution so you can return to balance and wholeness. Refer to Appendices C, E, and F for ways to discover your own beliefs.

Paul Solomon wisely explained to adults that "the beginning of parenting is to make a whole person, not of the child, but to make a whole person of yourself." Processing with yourself expands your own awareness about who you are. By examining yourself, you become better at helping children examine themselves.

LETTING GO OF PRECONCEPTIONS

It is wise to begin communications with an open heart and spirit by cultivating within yourself a willingness to let go. Let go of trying to control the outcome. The 5 Steps offers guidelines but the actual process will take its own course. By letting go, we release patterns of dominating the discussion with the younger person.

Adults have been accustomed to controlling children from the time they were infants. Since we tend to hold on, we become reluctant to let go. Yet by letting go, we help children learn how to become independent and gather feedback from their own experience. This paradox of caring for children while allowing freedom creates a delicate balance, a mystical dance between adult and child. It is a matter of learning the steps.

Beware of overstepping your bounds. For instance, adults feel their boundaries disturbed when others tell them what to feel and think. Then isn't the child also degraded when told what to feel and think by an adult?

In addition, adults can belittle children by talking excessively to them. To establish good boundaries, you can practice becoming aware of how much you speak and listen to youngsters.

The 5 Steps focus on how you can allow children to express themselves, rather than focusing on how to control children.

This does not mean you have to agree with whatever the child says. Adults still have their viewpoint and areas of responsibility.

Solutions will emerge naturally from using the 5 Steps. By being open-minded, you invite mutual understanding as the process unfolds. You can take a deep breath and relax. You no longer need to make something happen or feel compelled to change the situation for the child. You no longer have to rescue the child; instead you can help the child rescue herself.

TABLE 5.2
ADULT INVENTORY FOR STARTING THE 5 STEPS

Remember to:

- Determine whether you are in a positive state.

- Keep an open mind.

- Check if the child is willing to talk.

- Examine your own beliefs.

- Address practical needs, such as scheduling and having ample time to problem solve.

Avoid:

- Power struggles and lectures.

- Doing the 5 Steps when you are negative yourself.

- Having preconceptions of the child's problem and its solutions.

MORE RELEASING

To help children and yourself, consider difficult areas with your own parents. Any freeing of constricted relationships will help you now as the adult to guide yourself and others. It is hard to be there for a child when difficulties are coming up for you, the adult. Even if your parents are unavailable or no longer living, forgiveness, and releasing can still occur. To assist you, practice the 5 Steps on the issue(s), meditate, pray, use guided visualization, counseling or therapy. There are a few books on forgiveness listed in the bibliography also.

Remember the child takes longer to recognize her internal experience than the adult. Avoid interrupting the kid and giving her answers, depriving her of deeper learning and valuable insights. Give the child the chance to realize what she feels and thinks.

When you let go, the child can grow. And so do you.

CULTIVATING YOUR COMMUNICATION SKILLS

You have found your composure, you know who has the problem, and you are open to the child who wants your help. So now that you are prepared, what do you actually do? What is the adult's role in this process? What follows will give you cues on your role. The five tools you can use are questioning, listening, summarizing, guiding, and non-verbal language.

a) Questioning

As a guideline, try asking a question of the child rather than making a statement. Questioning stimulates the child to think and feel. The kid becomes more independent and responsible for herself. For instance, instead of stating to the child "You are feeling lonely," *ask* "What are you feeling?" Then the child, not the adult, develops the answer.

Allow for the silences.... Let you and the child explore issues, feelings, and thoughts at a pace that is comfortable for both of you. For instance, if she cannot find the words to fit the feeling, then at the right time ask about what she experiences. "Are you feeling lonely?"

Here are some more examples of giving questions to the child rather than answers. After the child has stated she does feel lonely, avoid offering an interpretation, such as "It sounds as though you think no one likes you." Instead ask "What do you think about being lonely?" (Remember underneath feelings are thoughts and beliefs, so explore what the child thinks about herself and the situation.)

A second example involves a child who has expressed the limiting belief that schoolwork is boring. Instead of telling the child, "There are many interesting things in school!" you can make questions that draw on her own experience and avoid the power struggle. For instance, you could ask "What is one thing you are interested in learning?" This might lead the child to find ways to make school more interesting.

Your questions lead to the child's answers.
Questions develop the child's awareness and
resources to solve her own problems.

Remember for questioning:

- Ask instead of tell.
- Allow for silences.

b) Listening

There was a man who put out notice that he would simply listen without interruption for five minutes to people who called him. Before long, the phone calls just continued without stopping.

People of all ages love to be heard. Yet our culture provides few opportunities for an individual to speak her mind without interference. Most people listen selectively, hearing only what they want, overanxious to speak themselves. It is a wonderful pleasure having someone really listen to you.

Listening deepens respect and caring for another. It requires the suspension of the listener's own speech and judgment. The person who is being heard can really open up, becoming expressive and intimate, able to release pent-up thoughts and feelings. Listening spurs insight and will help a person clear and integrate problems.

The Dale Carnegie Training notes in their national survey that "36% of respondents say listening to clients and establishing trust are the key elements of successful relationships."

Good listeners are highly valued and can be hard to find. One of the reasons people seek out a therapist is to find a good listener. And yet following another's words does not require special talents, just patience and practice. Listening asks one to be attentive to another, giving that person's words full attention.

Listening also helps a child to think. The kid knows by your attentiveness that her words are being heard and valued. This sharpens the child's focus, developing reasoning skills, and critical thinking abilities.

> *By your act of listening, you are helping the child to think better and become smarter.*

Practice listening to yourself as well as others. Tune into your own thoughts and feelings. Try suspending your criticisms and judgments. Hold a space to just hear what is being said without having to immediately respond. Be attentive to your inner, as well as outer, world. When you listen well, others develop trust in you and they will more deeply share their concerns with you.

Remember for listening:

- Be patient and attentive.
- Suspend judgments and criticisms.
- Practice on yourself and others regularly.

c)   Summarizing

Questioning and listening will help you summarize. The Dictionary tells us that a summary is "covering the main points briefly." When an adult summarizes the child's response, the younger person knows she has been heard. She receives validation for her thoughts and feelings, which counts for a great deal.

Remember to avoid putting words in the child's mouth. You might naturally expand or enhance what the child says, but the focus is one of summarizing what she has said. Beware of letting your summary turn into a speech. You can tell when you are longwinded by noticing the kid's eyes glaze over, tuning you out.

Summarizing supports the child by demonstrating you have followed what she has shared with you. The child has confided in you, and your summary builds her confidence. Like the skills of questioning and listening, summarizing leads to profound communication and trust.

Remember for summarizing:

- Accurately recount what the child has said.
- Keep your words to a minimum.

d) Guiding

The Dictionary informs us guiding means "to lead or conduct on the way, as to a place or through a region." Another definition connects guidance to a signpost or guidepost.

To add perspective on guidance, I would like to cite the ancient Chinese sage Lao Tsu. He noted that the good leader follows. He further stated that the effective leader seamlessly blends in with his followers, so they do not even know he has led them. The followers think they did it all themselves! These insights remind us that guiding can be a subtle process, a delicate work accomplished with a sensitive touch.

Adults naturally guide children. During the 5 Steps, you can use your experience to help kids at appropriate moments.

Areas for guidance include:

- Assisting the child with vocabulary.
- Giving relativity on choices.

- Offering realistic alternatives.
- Sharing and disclosing your own feelings and experiences.

Let's look closer at the last aspect of guiding listed above, namely, sharing and disclosing your own feelings and experiences. Guiding works well when you treat the person with respect and equality, however young the kid may be. Sharing what you understand from your own experience tells the child that you too have challenges. You too are vulnerable and human. You then establish connections, rather than relating as an omniscient elder bestowing wisdom on this troubled youth. Guiding based on sharing sends a powerful message to the child that you care and understand.

Sometimes the younger the child, the more guidance she may need. (Refer to Appendix A on the developmental stages of children.) Still remember that young children can be highly imaginative and creative. Do not dismiss their suggestions too readily. If the suggestion sounds unacceptable to you, return to questioning the child so she can see the consequences of her choice. For example, if the child suggests moving to a new house in order to have more space, you can ask her where can we get the money to do that.

Guidance can include being open to solutions from the child that you may not have considered. Whenever possible, give the kid's answers a chance to be tested. If you are unwilling to try them out, give her an explanation. Then ask for other choices. Again, work with the child to discover the answers. Avoid telling and dictating solutions - that old habit of the adult solving the problem solve for the child can easily slip into the experience.

Does this mean the adult becomes mute, unable to establish boundaries and values? Adults can certainly set limits where needed and work with children to find alternatives with acceptable standards.

Children learn responsibility by finding limits and then solving problems within those limits.

When the problem affects your life, tell that to the child. For example, if the solution costs you time and/or money, make that known and share your viewpoint. The next chapter addresses the adult's needs and concerns.

Children naturally seek adult guidance. Yet if you offer more advice than they seek, you can undermine their trust. Guidance works when it comes with intention and care. On the other hand, excessive advice causes kids to become overly-dependent or resistant to your help. Apply guidance like a spice: used sparingly it enhances, overused it deadens the experience.

Remember for guiding:

- Be aware of the child's age and maturity.
- Know your own boundaries and help the child with setting limits.
- Guide with humility, remembering to involve the child.

e) Establishing Rapport with Non-verbal Language

Another key to relating is non-verbal communication. This entails vocal expression (such as volume, tone, rhythm) and body movements (posture and expressions). It has been estimated that 38% of communication comes from the voice and 55% of the message comes from the body movement.

Awareness of how you speak and move can make the difference.

Regarding nonverbal messages, the need to be relatively calm when processing with the child has already been addressed. To further increase rapport, you can approximate the child's voice, volume, tone, and rhythm.

Communication also expresses itself through body position. Check out your body position right now. What does it say about your energy?

Relating to another person's body position opens up communication. This happens naturally when you establish rapport. Just observe friends talking in a restaurant and see how similar their positions are to each other.

Mirroring body posture helps you relate to the child. If you are lecturing a child, pointing your finger at them, standing above them, then rapport is absent. By contrast, when you sit similarly to the child, approximating her hand, arm, and head position, you get into the child's world and she opens up.

Matching another's breathing pattern also helps communication. If the child is disturbed, you can subtly help her calm down. Initially match her breath, then slow down and deepen your breathing. She will follow your lead when you have sufficiently gained rapport.

You might still be wondering why non-verbal matching is so helpful. An analogy might provide some insight. Take choosing an outfit to wear. Why is it preferable to pick matching clothes, that relate to color, form and occasion? Complimentary clothes selection creates harmony for the person wearing the clothes and those around her. Similarly, matching postures with another helps the communicator relate to the listener and feel more in tune with herself.

You can certainly mismatch postures, just like clothing, and still relate to another person. An interesting exercise is to intentionally mismatch your position with someone to see how it feels. But why not go for the harmony by matching non-verbal language, expanding the possibilities?

After matching non-verbal language, you will have established more trust with the child. The child will relate to you more. This then gives you an opportunity to lead the child with more positive postures, tone of voice, volume, and rhythm. If you have crossed your arms to match the child, you can unfold them after the child begins to open up. If you have been speaking rapidly to match the child, you can begin to slow down and soften your voice. Strategically leading the youngster works *after* you have gained the child's rapport.

Remember when relating with non-verbal language to match:

- Body position.

- Tone of voice, volume, and rhythm.

- Breathing.

So to review, here are the five key skills to help you process with children:

a) Asking questions.

b) Careful listening.

c) Summarizing the child's statements.

d) Guiding the child, by offering vocabulary and choices. (This part is best kept to a minimum.)

e) Matching body language, voice, and breathing (non-verbal communication).

FROM CRAWLING TO WALKING THE 5 STEPS

Here is a suggestion for beginning the 5 Steps with youngsters: just focus on asking questions and listening. Avoid giving the child any suggestions, solutions or answers. Be an investigative reporter, just trying to find out what happened.

For instance, if the child says he feels angry when a peer teases him, you can respond, "How come that makes you angry?" Don't assume you know why, even if you do. Give the child a chance to explore and explain his situation. Even though you know it is common to be angered by teasing, play reporter to find out what is really behind the story. Remember to use a sincere tone, free of any belitttling or judgment.

This may take a certain amount of patience and fortitude on your part, but the communication and problem solving results will be worth the effort. It can bring into balance tendencies to control and dominate the youngster.

If you get lost or stuck in the process, you can:

- Allow for silences.
- Remember the 5 Steps.
- Ask a question relevant to the situation.
- Listen neutrally.
- Maintain rapport through matching body language.
- Practice role playing about the problem.

You will naturally start to view things from the child's position. As you become accustomed to empathizing with the child and seeing things from her vantage point, processing becomes easier and more effective.

As you become more skilled with the 5 Steps, you will gain confidence in knowing when to offer guidance and how to pace the process. Life is a movement and a rest, and you will intuitively know when to be active and when to be receptive.

Yet there really is no formula to follow. Problems and children are complex. The 5 Steps is not meant as a cure-all for every situation and problem. At times it may not be suitable to use. You may have only partial results. You may have the steps go out of order. You may use only some of the steps. There are many possibilities. If you establish any rapport, feelings or beliefs, you have made some headway... and that can be a building block for the future.

To deepen the process, you can use the child's newfound positive belief in future situations. For instance, say the kid's new belief is "I can be included," that is, accepted by others. Then whenever it is appropriate, you can follow up by telling the child, "it sounds as if you were included in that situation." Using the kid's own words, "included" in this example, can reinforce the youngster's progress.

Take a moment to ask yourself: For how many years has the child's off beliefs been reinforced? Now a wonderful opportunity exists to change these problem-producing patterns. You can help redirect the youngster, strengthening the on beliefs and diminishing the off beliefs. In this way, you tap into a well spring of healing and growth for the child. Powerful long-term benefits can result.

You want to show that you care for the child. In each part of the 5 Steps, you can offer that caring through being with the child. You become a facilitator, a nurturer, a guide, so the child can reach his or her own potential.

The 5 Steps taught me that I no longer had to be the authority with all the answers. At first I felt awkward and confused, not knowing what to do. I had to let go of my need to lead and be in charge. After I relaxed with the process, I began to feel liberated, like finally arriving in the mountains and breathing the fresh air. What a release from the burden of playing the expert, teacher, and savior. I could be a person who was learning and exploring just like the child I was helping. I felt more human and the kids liked that. So did I.

CHAPTER SIX

Expressing Your Needs and Concerns

I hope you have not received the impression that you are supposed to sit through the process feeling as if you have a gag in your mouth. When you use the 5 Steps, you are taking on an active role by listening, questioning, summarizing, and guiding.

To look further at how adults express themselves, let's examine three possibilities: non-assertive behavior, aggressive behavior and assertive behavior. Also, keep in mind that behavior reflects beliefs and choices.

FALLING PREY TO NON-ASSERTIVE BEHAVIOR

Have you ever experienced a situation where you felt like you couldn't speak up and agreed to something you did not want?

This is non-assertive behavior. If you allow others to choose for you and consequently resent what happens, you are falling prey to non-assertiveness.

In his book *The Silence of the Heart,* Paul Ferrini examines the relationship between what we say and what we truly desire. "To say 'yes' or 'no' to another person is a clear communication. But to say 'no' and mean yes or to say 'yes' and mean no creates the conditions for abuse." Ferrini adds that this pattern causes abandonment and betrayal by others - and ultimately a betrayal of ourselves. This confusion can stem from gaps in our childhood development, dating back to toddlerhood and adolescence (see Appendix A on "Stages of Childhood Development").

For clear communication in the 5 Steps, you want to avoid becoming too passive. If the child's problem affects you, speak up. In truth, you choose to become a victim by going along with another's decisions when the issues affect you. Non-assertive behavior reveals itself by feelings of anxiety, inhibition, and hurt. After you acted against your better judgment, you feel guilty, angry, resentful.

For example, if a son has a problem finding transportation, the parent needs to express how much transporting she chooses to do for her son. The adult has practical matters, her time and her own preferences to consider. A non-assertive response might have the adult doing frequent driving and sabotaging her other responsibilities and interests.

The image of the good wife "biting her tongue" comes to mind, doing the husband's bidding without expressing any wishes of her own. In our case, the adult needs to beware of the "bitten tongue" syndrome while helping the child. Take time to probe the beliefs that keep you down and victimized.

RUNNING OVER OTHERS WITH AGGRESSIVE BEHAVIOR

The father chides the son, "You don't have to watch the show you want. Give your sister a turn!" Although the father may be trying to help, this is aggressive adult behavior. Aggression involves depreciating others, choosing for someone else, achieving goals by putting down others. In our example, the father disrespected the son, who felt he wasn't given a choice in the matter. The son also felt hurt and defensive. The father's good intention was overrun by his aggressive approach, in effect seizing the remote control in the situation.

As this text has pointed out, much of adult interaction with children has traditionally been through an aggressive approach. Adults can easily transgress their natural guidance roles and become more like harsh bosses than attentive caretakers.

The adult orders of "my way or the highway" create a bleak landscape for children to travel. Be watchful for aggressively imposing solutions that result in denying the child a voice in the matter. Children can end up feeling quite lonely and lost.

Aggressive behavior indicates limiting beliefs are at work. To discover roots of aggression, you can ask yourself these questions:

- Do you confuse controlling others with responsibility and safe boundaries?

- Are you sufficiently flexible with yourself and others?

- What do your words, tone of voice, and body language say about you?

BALANCING WITH ASSERTIVE BEHAVIOR

We all know how difficult it can be to stand up for ourselves, especially when we are in the minority.

It is a satisfying feeling to express yourself. You become self-enhancing, connected to the issues that concern you. If non-assertive behavior is a stagnant atmosphere, and

---

SHAME AND REMORSE

As an adult, you might experience a twinge of remorse at aggressions from your past. I have experienced shame about some of my own behavior, but I try to understand that I did the best I could at the time. Now that I know better, I can do better.

When experiencing such intense emotions as shame, you can intentionally release feelings by:

- Concentrating on the breath.

- Affirming "I now release that behavior and am free to move on with my life."

- Using prayer and spiritual guidance.

aggressive behavior is a cyclone, then assertive behavior is like a gentle summer breeze.

In the 5 Steps, there are times when the child brings up issues that directly concern you. You need to assert yourself when the kid's problem affects your responsibilities, time, and money. Find alternative solutions that are mutually acceptable to you and the child. Develop "a willingness to stay open to a solution that honors both sides," as Paul Ferrini describes.

A common situation I have seen play out involves a child wanting her mother to buy an expensive CD player - a purchase that would definitely affect the mother's pocketbook. To put things straight, Mom asserts herself. She tells her daughter directly that she cannot afford the expensive player. At the time, the mother was shopping for a discounted vacuum, a purchase that would serve the whole family.

Using the 5 Steps, they came to a solution where the daughter could earn money over time for the equipment she wanted. Mom also helped shift her child's belief from "I *never* get what I want" to "I *sometimes* get what I want."

The 5 Steps work well when the adult is neutral and open. The kid then has the opportunity to gain confidence and insight. When directly affected by the child's problem, you can talk about your needs as a part of the process. If the kid's solution is to sleep overnight at a friend's house that you think is unsupervised, you can say, "I don't feel you would be safe in that environment. What else could you do?"

The child will generally look for alternatives when she feels listened to and respected. Since she is being included in the decision-making, she is likely to respect the adult's concerns and boundaries.

Let's examine further how boundaries and trust affect assertiveness.

Assertiveness and Boundaries

Part of determining boundaries involves defining what is acceptable. Remember that children sometimes like to explore wild, dangerous, and impractical solutions. You need not react or shut off the child at that point. The key is to remain calm and explore what may be the child's far-fetched solutions. Give the child a chance to think through her choices.

For instance, the child might have a restrictive belief about school being too difficult. Her solutions may be cheating or giving up. Allow her to express these possibilities and explore the consequences without adding any judgments. Most of us have thought of cheating or quitting school, but that does not mean we would actually do it. When you respect the youngster by allowing her expression of antisocial possibilities, she will naturally arrive at a new understanding. The child will come to realize that there are better solutions.

You do not have to convince the child - this may just breed argument and resistance. Coercing someone undermines communication... and indicates aggressive behavior. Let the child discover the truth for herself. The communication process will give clearer definition to standards, boundaries, and rules. You are still responsible for setting limits. Society holds you accountable and you have your standards to maintain.

The way you set up these limits is important. For instance, if the child trashes your belongings, then *your* boundaries are being violated. It is time to establish limits and consequences.

Here are two ways to set up boundaries for the child:

- Listen to the child's suggestions for the consequences of her misbehavior. But, before agreeing to them, be sure they are reasonable.

    Example: Yes, I agree with you Kim: you can pay for the broken window out of your allowance.

- Implement your own standards, making sure you carefully explain the reasons and define the boundaries. Use this option to revise the child's suggestion and strengthen her sense of boundaries.

    Example: From now on Kim, you cannot play ball in the front yard because it is too near the windows; and you will need to pay for the broken window out of your allowance.

Exploring boundaries helps show the child how to choose safely and wisely.

Assertiveness and Trusting the Child

It also helps to believe that the child will make good decisions and that she will learn from her mistakes. By trusting the youngster, you help her adopt the belief to trust herself. That's effective guidance.

As the Bayards write in *How to Deal with Your Acting-Up Teenager*, you can love a person for her decision-making ability. The ability to respond contributes to a person's uniqueness. It empowers the child when you support her ability to decide for herself. Believing in the child helps her believe in herself.

Table 6 can help you identify degrees of assertiveness. It shows how behaviors reflect balance. On the one side, non-assertive behavior weakens, undermines, and evades. On the other side, aggressive behavior coerces, overrides, and destroys. You find balance with assertive behavior, allowing for right action in the moment.

Non-assertive behaviors include mumbling, hands over face, no eye contact. Aggressive behaviors include cussing, shouting, and threatening gestures. When you choose to be in the assertive mode, your body is alert but relaxed. You direct and focus your words. You listen and stand up for yourself. To follow up, note your own assertiveness on your next problem solving session.

A note: When the child's problem does not affect you - your responsibilities, time, and money - then it may be easier to do the 5 Steps. In this event, you are less involved personally, which makes detachment and trusting the child easier.

FINDING THE BALANCE

Your recommended tools - listening, questioning, summarizing, guiding, and non-verbal language - take an active, assertive approach to bring positive results. Allow each situation's uniqueness to present its own solutions through the process. Then everybody's needs can be addressed.

To take care of others, you want to
be sure you have taken care of yourself.

Keeping this balance poises you to help the youngster who can really use your help.

TABLE 6
BODY LANGUAGE SIGNALS: NON-ASSERTIVE (WEAK),
AGGRESSIVE (TOO STRONG), ASSERTIVE (BALANCED),

POSTURE: Non-Assertive	Assertive	Aggressive
slumped	erect and relaxed	rigid, tense
shifting often	still, few shifts	jerky shifts or planted in place

GESTURES: Non-Assertive	Assertive	Aggressive
shoulder shrugs	hands open, relaxed	clenched fists or points
frequent head nods	occasional head nods	sweeping arms, sharp nods

FACIAL EXPRESSION: Non-Assertive	Assertive	Aggressive
chews lower lip	relaxed face	tight lips
shows anger with averted eyes, guilty look	shows anger with straightforward look	shows anger with scowl or bared teeth

VOICE: Non-Assertive	Assertive	Aggressive
quiet, soft higher pitch	resonant, firm, pleasant	steely quiet or loud harsh
start and stop	comfortable delivery	measured or rapid delivery

The child has needs and so does the adult. The different generations have much in common, providing wonderful opportunities to learn from each other.

For expressing your needs and concerns remember to:

- Avoid going along with others when you don't really want to.

- Avoid running over others with your own desires and needs.

- Stand up for yourself, squarely telling kids when your time, money, and responsibility is affected by them.

- Know your own boundaries and help the child create good boundaries.

- Discover ways to support the child's decision-making abilities.

- Find your own On beliefs.

Behavior reflects a person's thoughts and feelings. And underlying thoughts and feelings are beliefs. Off beliefs prompt aggressive and non-assertive behavior. On beliefs support assertive behavior.

As you learn skills to act assertively, your thoughts and feelings come into alignment with your actions. Getting thru to kids naturally follows.

CHAPTER SEVEN

Putting It All Together

This chapter shows you two examples of what an entire 5-step process looks like. The first actual transcription comes from a talk between a mother and her eleven year old son. In both transcriptions, the names of the children have been changed.

Bear in mind there are many variations of the 5-step process. Your experiences will create your own material and approach. It is not about getting it right; it's about getting in the flow, being in the moment. Naturally the age of the child and the uniqueness of each person come into play.

EXAMPLE: DAN AND HIS MOTHER

Step 1:   Mother: What's the problem?
Problem

Dan: My teacher is reading a boring book. I fall asleep in class.

Step 2:
Feelings

Mother: How do you feel when she reads that book?

Dan: I feel bored and like I need to do something... instead of sit there.

Step 3:
Off Belief

Mother: So that makes school boring.

Dan: Yes.

Step 4: play
"Change" to
On Belief

Mother: What could you do to be more interested and alert?

Dan: I could go to bed earlier and eat lunch.

Mother: Yes, that's a good idea.

Dan: I could ask if I could read. Popcorn read.

Questioning

Mother: What's that?

Dan: That's when people take turns and call on the next person to read.

Summarizing
Step 5:
Future

Mother: So you can ask to read aloud part of the time. And you can get more sleep at night and eat lunch. So, what

do you see yourself doing next time
your teacher is reading?

Dan: Following along and sitting up
straight.

Mother: What color do you see?

Dan: Yellow.

Mother: What sounds do you hear?

Dan: Sighs.

Questioning   Mother: Sighs because you're paying
attention?

Dan: Yes.

Mother: How do you think we did
finding a solution to your problem?

Dan: I think we did well.

Summarizing   Mother: So now that you're going to eat
right, sleep right, sit up, and follow
along, how do you think school will be?

Dan: A little more enjoyable.

I think you could discern the transformation going on with
Dan. Even though he concluded with saying school would be
"a little more enjoyable," the promise of deep change was

evident. He creatively and appropriately problem solved, took responsibility for himself, and brightened his outlook on school. Time will allow him to integrate this experience and experience further growth.

After concluding the above process, the mother went on to say how impressed she was at the solutions Dan found. She discovered, like many adults who do the 5 Steps, that her son was more resourceful than she realized. And Mom did not have to shoulder so much responsibility for his problem... a welcome relief.

Dan expressed how proud he was of himself. He was confident he could cope with his problems. He now had more tools available after the positive processing experience. Knowing that challenges still lay ahead, Dan could better handle it... and enjoy himself more.

THE 5 STEPS WITH DAN AND HIS MOTHER

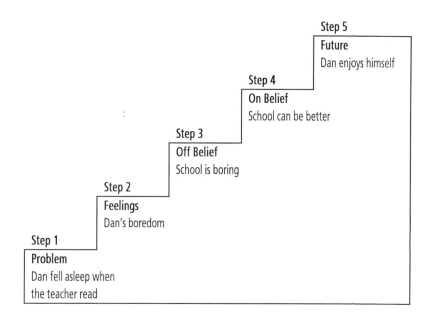

Step 5
Future
Dan enjoys himself

Step 4
On Belief
School can be better

Step 3
Off Belief
School is boring

Step 2
Feelings
Dan's boredom

Step 1
Problem
Dan fell asleep when the teacher read

EXAMPLE: CINDY AND HER MOTHER

The second transcription of the 5 Steps occurred between a mother and her seventeen year old daughter.

Step 1: *Problem*	Mother: What's been the problem?
Step 2: *Feelings* *about problem*	Cindy: Don't you think I'm old enough to have my own room? I'm seventeen and I have to share it with my little sister.
	Mother: How do you feel about not having your own room?
	Cindy: Frustrated. It's hard! I can't do anything with my friends because my tag-along sister is there.
Step 3: Keep *probing feelings,* *and look for the* *Off Belief*	Mother: What's causing the frustration?
	Cindy: I don't get any privacy. [Off belief established; notice it's phrased as an absolute, using 'any'.] She hears my telephone conversations, mimics me and sometimes goes through my stuff.
Mother plays *"Change" to*	Mother: We only have a two bedroom apartment. There is

find new belief	no other place to make a bed. How could you get some privacy?
	Cindy: We could get a bigger apartment.
Sharing without arguing	Mother: I wish I had a bigger job. Were there any times you have had privacy?
Step 4: On Belief reluctance at first	Cindy: Some, very few [here is the on belief: I've had some privacy]. When she's at day care or at her friend's house, then I can talk to my friends without interruption.
Mom reinforces on belief and develops it	Mother: There is some privacy. How else could you have more private time?
	Cindy: Sometimes I want to be with my friends or study and concentrate for a test.
	Mother: Have you talked with your sister about this?
	Cindy: Sometimes, but she doesn't really listen.
The questions build on the positive	Mother: What happens when she does listen?

Daughter finds
solutions

Cindy: Sometimes I tell her if she leaves me alone for two hours, I'll take her out for ice cream or a movie.... I guess I could do it more often.

Mother: Can you find privacy anywhere else beside your bedroom?

Cindy: I could study at the library.

Summarizing
and guiding

Mother: So there are two alternatives. Offer her rewards, she'd like that coming from you. And I could help you out by giving you money for movies or ice cream. And secondly, when you go to the library I think she'll understand. She'd like her own private time and you could have your quiet time...

Step 5:
Future

Mother: What do you see happening in the future about private times?

Cindy: I feel more at peace. I'm by myself.

Mother: What color do you associate with that?

Cindy: I see white. I'm more

family closeness
developing

peaceful with myself or with my friends. I feel happier, calmed down. Sometimes I miss my sister.

Mother: What do you think about more privacy?

Cindy: I think this will help a lot.

Mom summarizes
and expresses
her feelings

Mother: I feel proud we could talk this out. You were able to let me understand how you were feeling, rather than you just brooding over it. This is better than you getting mad at your sister, and then I get mad. I'll talk with your sister too. If you open up to her, she might understand more. This makes me happier and makes our household a lot happier; we can all talk to each other.

Cindy: I feel a lot better. I know I can get more of what I want.

The 5 Steps usually plays out more as a dance than a straightforward march to the finish line. Mom takes a step, then the daughter moves. Mom carefully follows each movement of her daughter, careful not to lead too much, following her daughter's pace. It can be quite an artistic progression, where the rhythm changes with each thought and feeling expressed. And when the two are in step, a wonderful movement unfolds.

THE 5 STEPS WITH CINDY AND HER MOTHER

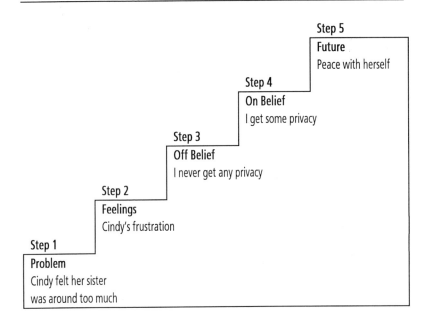

The mother kept her patience with Cindy. She did not become defensive, even if she was uncomfortable with not being able to provide a larger living space for her family. She kept on listening, questioning, and summarizing. By empathizing, she avoided confrontational language or put downs. She did not tell the daughter the answers either, though the mother did offer to help by giving money to Cindy so she could take out her younger sister. Her mother offered herself as a resource, avoiding becoming a savior or authoritarian.

The mom communicated with the daughter without having to dominate or control. She was still the parent with her responsibilities; but she gave her daughter the dignity and freedom to solve her own problem. Cindy was free to find solutions to having more privacy with the wonderful support of her mother.

The family's self-esteem blossomed as they drew closer together by the experience. Such deep expressiveness opens up more possibilities in the future. Everyone grows from the experience.

A note: Nine months after this recorded exchange, Cindy shared with me that her relations with her mother had improved. "We don't argue as much any more. We talk things out."

CHAPTER EIGHT

A Quick Reference to the Five Steps

This chapter compiles suggestions on how to use the 5 Steps. It can serve both as a review and a troubleshooting guide for the process.

SUGGESTIONS FOR STEP 1 THROUGH STEP 5:

- Check your own state of mind for your feelings, thoughts, and beliefs.

- Begin the process with an open mind and suspend preconceptions throughout the process.

- If possible, allow enough time to complete the process (possibly five to thirty minutes).

- You will relate better to the child by approximating the child's posture. If she sits, you sit. If she stands and folds her arms, you do the same. Relating to the child's body language establishes rapport. After you gain rapport, you can lead the child into more open, relaxed body language.

- Allow the child to say as much as possible. The adult need only offer minimal guidance and words. The talk can also open up other issues and meaningful discussions between adult and child.

- Listen carefully for the child's feelings, thoughts, and beliefs. Allow the child to really express himself. The child will feel your care and respect when you closely hear his words.

- Use the child's key words when communicating with him. But be careful not to mimic or be too repetitive with his own words.

- Avoid trying to "fix" things for the child or rescue him, depriving him of learning.

- Be concrete, using terms he understands. The younger the child, the simpler the language. He may need help articulating thoughts and feelings, but keep it simple.

- Allow for periods of silence in the communication. Processing can take time to unfold. Children need more time to understand their internal world than adults. Be patient.

- The 5 Steps can have positive results even if you do not use all the steps or go out of sequence.

FOR STEP 1: THE PROBLEM

- You need to be calm enough yourself to process with the child. Take some deep breaths or wait until you can talk and listen with a neutral open attitude.

- The child needs to be willing to speak about the problem. If the child is too disturbed or in denial about the problem, find another time to process. The right time may be minutes or days later.

- If the child's problem directly affects you, share your thoughts and feelings with the child. Be aware when the situation concerns your responsibility, time or money. Then work out a solution with the child that is mutually acceptable to both of you.

FOR STEP 2: FEELINGS

- Develop a vocabulary for feelings. Study and memorize feeling words. Use Appendix B as a reference.

- Practice using "I feel..." statements on a regular basis.

FOR STEP 3 AND 4: ON AND OFF BELIEFS

- Recognize negative beliefs by hearing a demanding tone of

voice and absolute words such as "never," "always," "everything," "totally," "nothing."

- Remember to have the child discover the solution whenever possible. This way he is likely to carry it out and internalize the learning.

- Ask the child for information and solutions, rather than telling him. The child will generally arrive at the solutions himself from your questions. Careful listening to the child will help him concentrate and think for himself.

- Ask the child about the short and long term consequences of his belief.

- There are ten core beliefs centered on value, security, performance, control, love, autonomy, justice, belonging, others, and standards (see Appendix C for details).

- Be sure to phrase the newfound belief in the positive, such as "I am honest" rather than "I don't lie."

- Develop strategies for helping the child actualize the new belief. Suggestions include role playing, journalling, and artwork.

FOR STEP 5: FUTURE VISION

- To establish and develop the future vision, use images and colors, sounds and words, body sensations, and, when applicable, taste and smell.

- If you note the child relies on one sense more than another, appeal to that more developed sense. For instance, if the child is more attuned to his body ask him what sensations he experiences in the future vision. "When you see yourself on the playground around those kids, how is your body feeling?"

- If the kid draws a blank, use the prompting words "*what if.*" "What if you could hear the sounds, or see the picture or feel the sensations?" This encourages the kid's imagination and reinforces the new belief.

FOLLOW-UP TO THE 5 STEPS:

- Practicing the 5 Steps will develop your ability to recognize common belief patterns. You will sometimes sense the underlying belief system with your experience and be able to help the child find new positive outlooks.

- After processing, reinforce the child's newfound belief. Keep referring to the new outlook, using the child's own words when appropriate. For instance, the parent can remind the child, "I know you can learn from your mistakes" (an example of an on belief).

- Realize it may take time for the child to integrate the new belief. Although the old belief may still be there, you can find ways to remind her of the new understanding. This will strengthen the on belief.

- Adults can examine their own beliefs and see how they affect themselves and their children.

CHAPTER NINE

Testing
the Process

This chapter gives you a chance to practice what you have learned. The idea is to take a child's problem and apply the 5 Steps to it. Doing this exercise can be an important follow through and will help you integrate what you have learned.

To find a subject, interview a kid about a difficulty. Take notes or record the session if you choose. If a child is unavailable, use your memory and imagine some problem encountered by a child you know. You may need to rely on your own educated guesses to fill in some of the parts.

Step 1 - Identifying the problem. In your notebook, write out a problem the child has experienced. Be descriptive, trying to present what is happening without analysis. For example, here is a description of a kid's problem: "A girl in school is picking

on me. She keeps making fun of me and every day won't stop."
Avoid interpreting, just stay with the facts. Don't write that
the girl was mean and cruel unless the child with the problem
actually says that about the girl who teased her.

Identify the Problem. Use a separate paper or notebook to
record your answers for this step and those that follow.

Step 2 - Feelings about the problem:
Note the feelings
associated with the problem you earlier identified in Step 1 of
the process. If you are working directly with a child ask her
about the feelings the problem brings up for her. If the child is
unavailable, remember you can use your own imagination to
find out possible feelings experienced in the situation.

Here is an example of writing about feelings that follows up
on the previously cited problem, regarding the girl being
ridiculed by a peer. "I felt frustrated because I tried to talk to
her and she won't listen. I also am afraid she might hurt me."

Record the *Feelings about the Problem.*

Step 3 - Off Belief.
Continuing with the original example,
let's examine thoughts behind the child's feelings of
frustration and fear. You can ask the kid about what she thinks
of her problem and the troubling situation. The child may
have concerns about her safety. If this is the case, take it
seriously without becoming more alarmed than necessary. Yet
it is still good to note that the child's beliefs about safety may
be contributing to her as a target for another. The kid's
response might go something like, "I don't know what to do. *I
can't stand being picked on.*" (The italicized part notes the
restrictive off belief.)

Record and *Identify the Off Beliefs* associated with the
problem and feelings you outlined in step 1 and step 2.

Step 4 - On Belief. So now it's time to find and write out a more positive belief. Through a reasoning process play "Truth," "Consequences" or "Change." With the problem you used in the first three steps, find the truth behind the belief ("Truth"). Or follow the undesirable results of an off belief ("Consequences"). Or simply change the belief, opening it up to more possibilities ("Change").

Finding an on belief needs some adult guidance. So for this section, you can record your questions as well as the child's responses. Let's follow our example from the last step, which established the kid's off belief. The next step of the process uses the "Change" approach to transform the child's restrictive belief "I can't stand being picked on." Here is an example using a question and answer format:

Adult: It sounds like you feel real uncomfortable when that girl picks on you. Have you talked to her about it?

Child: Yes, she just won't listen.

Adult: What could you do to change things?

Child: Well, I could take a different recess time than her.

Adult: Is that possible?

Child: I think so.

Adult: When does she pick on you?

Child: When I'm by myself.

Adult: So what else could you do besides be by yourself at recess or when you walk home?

Child: I could be with my friends. Or you could pick me up after school sometimes.

Adult: That's a possibility. We could also all talk with the principal about the situation, and include her parents.

Child: Okay, as long as I don't have to sit next to her.

Adult: All right. So what do you think about your situation now?

Child: It's better. *I think I'll be able to handle it* [when being teased].
(The italics represent the new on belief.)

Record the *New On Belief.*

Step 5 - **Future Vision:** So now it is time to write about the newly conceived future. Use sight, sound, feelings, and possibly taste or smell. To follow our example from the prior steps: the child associates the color, sights, and sounds of accepting not getting what he wants. The kid sees herself being more easygoing in the situation and others responding in kind. Note how at ease her body feels. Are there tastes or scents associated?

To conclude our sample situation, a future vision would be: "I see myself playing with my friends at recess. The other girl leaves me alone [sight]. I hear myself laughing and having fun with my friends [sound]. My body relaxes and my breathing is calm. I feel better [sensations, feelings]."

Record the *Future Vision*.

Take time to review what you wrote and what you learned. You can also record your thoughts and any questions in your notebook. Return to these writings when you feel the time is right.

CHAPTER TEN

A New Beginning

So, when the shoe fits
the foot is forgotten
when the belt fits
the belly is forgotten
when the heart is right
"for" and "against" are forgotten.

- CHUANG TZU

Now you have a powerful framework for adult child communications. By using skills such as listening, building rapport, questioning, allowing, and summarizing, you set up new ways to relate. The door opens for deeper relationships to enter.

Children learn to think for themselves and come to good decisions. In touch with their thoughts and feelings, youngsters can help themselves and others. Adolescence, then, need not be a time for extreme rebellion, destruction, and violence.

A kid is likely to make good choices when he has problem solving strategies and liberating beliefs. On the other hand, a child who has been expected to be too obedient may have problems thinking independently and taking care of himself by the time adulthood arrives.

Raised by a controlling parent, the adolescent can find a gang or anti-social group attractive. The kid then transfers his unquestioning obedience from parent to peer. Or the teenager seeks other peers to bolster his own rebellion.

Strains on family relationships can lead the young to find gangs attractive. Gangs mirror the old dominating, controlling models of authority. Children can become desperate for power, respect, and belonging. Some find it in gangs who so readily punish those who disobey and disrespect them. These tactics extend the punitive ways that children learned from adults. Many a gang member's limiting beliefs - about justice, honesty and inclusion - began long before the person ever entered a gang. The time to correct children's erroneous beliefs is in early childhood, with the youngsters participating in their own solutions.

NOW YOU CAN MAKE A DIFFERENCE

Congratulations! You have taken the time to study and interact with the Getting Thru to Kids material. You have chosen to make a difference. You know more about kids as well as yourself. This manual is a tool to add to any others you may have. The journey becomes more exciting and fulfilling.

You now have the resources to reach your goals. You know how to:

- Find the underlying source of problems, limiting beliefs, and discover uplifting beliefs to transform the problem.

- Empower kids to take more responsibility and find effective problem solving strategies.

- Help kids develop their thoughts and feelings.

- Identify and express your own adult needs and concerns to children.

- Establish more trust between you and kids.

- Change power struggles into communication breakthroughs.

- Turn kids' negative outlooks to positive ones.

- Increase kids' higher level thinking abilities.

- Improve children's listening as well as your own.

By putting this knowledge into practice, you become a better communicator. Your awareness continues to expand. You now have tools to create profound changes. This can have a powerful rippling effect to uplift others and the whole of society.

It's time to instill more resources into the bigger picture: how to build children's self-esteem. This involves having kids' needs met, such as safety, security, belonging, respect, and reaching their potential. To create heartening possibilities, you can establish an environment of openness and encouragement with youngsters, such as the kind you have been exploring in this book.

Self-esteem in children and families builds on the communication skills in *Getting Thru To Kids*. Self-esteem, open communication, and problem solving help youngsters deal with the complexities of growing up and actually becoming an adult, however long that takes. For many of us, it takes a while.

The information in *Getting Thru To Kids* aspires to create a more loving environment. Love comes with boundaries but without conditions.

As you connect with young people, they can feel the support and security when you are there for them. Trust and understanding grow as children are seen *and* heard. A true dialogue occurs.

By opening your beliefs and vision of the future, you come to realize your own intrinsic wholeness. The 5 Steps leads to this wonderful sense of inner knowing. You deeply connect with yourself and who you are. And as you embrace yourself, you can embrace others. Each step of the process affirms the worth of the participants, regardless of age. You are never too young, or too old, to value yourself. And when you value who you are, problems get solved.

Following the 5-step process takes you on a journey both inwardly to self-discovery and outwardly to rapport with others. You can use this book as a map, helping to prepare for the expected and unexpected turns along the way. I invite you to send me a note sharing some of your triumphs with a fellow communicator and problem solver.

Phillip Mountrose

Table of Appendices and Other Back Matter

Stages of Childhood Development

As you noticed in the subtitle of this volume, the problem solving is for children ages 6 to 18. Be aware, though, that children at younger ages can still benefit from the material explored in this book. It depends on their maturity and your relationship to them.

Depending on the kid's current age, the child has gone through different stages of development and has some further stages to complete. Each stage occurs at roughly certain ages and pertains to certain tasks for a child's growth. Wherever a child doesn't fulfill these learning stages, developmental gaps remain, creating difficulties as the child grows older. This accounts for much of the problems we have as adults - leftover issues from childhood.

The following reference material on childhood development can help you:

- Associate the child's age with his current developmental stage.

- Understand that the child may have troubles stemming from incomplete development at an earlier stage, dating back as early as birth in some cases.

- Take into account that what is incomplete from one stage will carry over and affect the later stages of development. For instance, if the child did not get her needs met at the infant stage - such as feeding, cleaning, and resting - related issues and belief systems may show up as the child ages. Thus the child may have trust issues around basic survival needs. This may in turn incite the kid's rebelliousness during the adolescent stage.

- Realize that these particular issues can be found in adults including yourself.

- Seek new beliefs to bridge gaps in a child's development. The 5 Steps can pinpoint areas where the child feels inadequate. It also provides new outlooks for future growth.

A good source to use for this material is Cathryn L. Taylor's *The Inner Child Workbook*. Also note in the following information that the age ranges for each stage are approximations.

INFANT STAGE (0 to 18 months) - symbiotic with mother, attachment.

Potential Challenges:

- Fear of closeness, concerns with abandonment.
- Needing, but fear of physical affection.
- Inability to trust.

TODDLER STAGE (18 months to 3 years) - independence from parent, exploring.

Potential Challenges:

- Inability to say no.
- Inability accepting being told no.
- Difficulty expressing feelings.
- Feeling smothered if someone gets too close.

EARLY SCHOOL AGE (3 to 7 years) - consciously manipulating environment, moving from mother to father.

Potential Challenges:

- Awkward about body.
- Highly critical of self and others.
- Perfectionist.

GRADE SCHOOL STAGE (7 to 13) - away from parents, care about others, developing skills and abilities.

Potential Challenges:

- Self-conscious in social gatherings.
- Trouble completing projects.
- Self-discipline.

ADOLESCENT STAGE (14 to 19) - realize growing up is irreversible, need for control, rebellious, judgmental, black and white thinking.

Potential Challenges:

- Substance use or destructive behavior.
- Self-conscious about appearance.
- Inability to stand up for self.
- Controlling and critical of another's behavior.

Developing a Vocabulary for Feelings

This is a list of words that describe feelings. It can help you on step two, the feelings, or anywhere you need to find a word to describe feelings. Most children have a limited vocabulary when it comes to knowing and applying these words. Not surprisingly, these words may be absent from adults' language too.

- Angry
- Apathetic
- Blissful
- Confident

- Anxious
- Ashamed
- Bored
- Confused

- Creative
- Determined
- Disappointed
- Enthusiastic
- Exasperated
- Frustrated
- Grieving
- Hopeful
- Indifferent
- Meditative
- Inspired
- Joyful
- Negative
- Optimistic
- Passive
- Regretful
- Resentful
- Satisfied
- Sick
- Threatened
- Withdrawn

- Depressed
- Disbelieving
- Enraged
- Envious
- Frightened
- Grateful
- Helpless
- Hurt
- Insecure
- Miserable
- Jealous
- Lonely
- Obstinate
- Pained
- Puzzled
- Relieved
- Sad
- Shocked
- Sympathetic
- Triumphant

Discovering Different Core Beliefs

Matthew McKay and Patrick Fanning, authors of several books on communication and self-esteem, have identified ten general areas that generate core beliefs: Value, Security, Performance, Control, Love, Autonomy, Justice, Belonging, Others, and Standards.

Take time to answer the following questions under each belief category so you can examine and familiarize yourself with your own beliefs. You will probably find enhancing as well as limiting beliefs. This will give you the awareness to know where your strengths and weaknesses lie. Be open to what you find and avoid judging yourself.

Beliefs about Value have to do with your *worthiness.*

- How much do you value your needs?

- How interesting and unique do you think you are?

- How attractive are you (physically, mentally, emotionally, spiritually)?

Reflect now on your responses to the above questions. Write a statement in your notebook about your beliefs regarding your Value.

Beliefs about Security have to do with how *safe* you perceive you are.

- How safe do you feel the world is?

- Are you confident you will survive and be safeguarded?

- Or do you think disasters are lurking around the corner?

- How well do you think you can protect yourself?

- Are you confident about your health?

- Are you willing to take some risks?

- How secure are you about money and finances?

- Do you feel good about taking care of yourself and loved ones?

- Are you willing to explore new places and break old routines in order to grow?

Reflect on your responses to the above questions. Write down a statement about your belief(s) regarding Security.

Beliefs about Performance center around how *competent* you believe you are.

- Do you feel you perform many tasks well?

- Do you feel some things come easily for you?

- Do you trust your own judgment?

- Do you get concerned about others being more competent than you?

- Are you willing to learn new skills? Think of some new skills you learned in the past year.

- How well do you perform under stress?

- Are you satisfied with most of your decisions?

Consider your responses to the above questions. Write a statement about your belief(s) concerning Performance.

Control beliefs have to do with perceiving yourself as *powerful* and able to *act* and *respond.*

- How much control do you have of your life?

- Can you take care of your own problems?

- Can you handle most events in your life?

- How well do you deal with the unexpected?

- How well do you govern your impulses?

- How easily do you go out of control, giving in to explosive or damaging impulses?

- How much do you control your anger and express it appropriately?

- Do you see yourself as a victim of circumstances?

Consider your responses to the above questions. Write a statement on your beliefs about Control.

Core beliefs about Love have to do with *giving and receiving love, caring, and nurturing.*

- How loved and cared for do you feel?

- Do you have at least one satisfying intimate relationship?

- How deep are your relationships?

- Do you nurture others?

- How much do you nurture yourself? Think of examples like walks, baths, treats, etc.

- Are you afraid of being abandoned, that a loved one will die or reject you?

- Do you get the care and attention you need?

- Are there people you can count on for support and advice?

Consider your responses to the above questions. Write a statement on your belief(s) about Love.

Autonomy beliefs have to do with your *independence*.

- How self-reliant are you?

- Can you disagree with others and still feel all right?

- How well do you function on your own?

- Do you enjoy spending time with yourself?

- Do you tend to please others, putting their needs before your own?

- Do you stand up for yourself and your ideas?

- How well do you make your own wants and needs known?

Consider your responses to the above questions. Write a statement about your belief(s) on Autonomy.

Beliefs about Justice have to do with how *fairly* you are treated.

- How well do you handle not getting your way or what you want?

- Do you believe things tend to work out, in the end?

- Do you feel you are the exception to the rule, not needing to attend to restrictions put on others?

- Do you feel you are usually treated fairly?

- Do you tend to expect the worst?

- How accepting are you of how things turn out?

Consider your responses to the above questions. Write a statement about your belief(s) regarding Justice.

Beliefs regarding Belonging have to do with how *connected* you are to others: those close to you, acquaintances and people in general.

- How much of a sense of belonging do you have to your family?

- How much do you connect with your community?

- How much do you feel connected to the Earth and humanity?

- Do you feel like an outsider?

- Do you usually feel included by others when you desire?

- How much do you see that you have in common with others?

Consider your responses to the above questions. Write a statement about your belief(s) concerning Belonging.

Beliefs about Others have to do with *trust* and *positive relationships*.

- Do you feel many people can be trusted?

- Do you feel many people would like to hurt you or take advantage of you?

- Do you feel you generally need to be on guard with people?

- Do you give people the benefit of the doubt?

- Do you think people tend to break promises and lie?

Consider your responses to the above questions. Write a statement on your belief(s) regarding Others.

The final category concerns beliefs about Standards.

Standards that are reasonable and flexible help one be *compassionate* and *effective.*

- Do you set reasonable standards for yourself?

- Do you keep your reasonable standards without being rigid?

- Are you generally satisfied with what you do?

- Do you forgive yourself for failure?

- Are you a perfectionist, needing to be the best at whatever you do?

- Are your goals achievable? you accept your imperfections?

- Do you tend to push yourself, sometimes damaging your health or relationships?

- Is it okay for you to make mistakes?

- Are your rules for yourself very black and white, rigid and inflexible?

Reflect on your answers to the above questions. Write a statement on your belief(s) about Standards.

GAINING CONFIDENCE BY SEEING THE BIG PICTURE

Beliefs are very powerful. They orient us to the world and

determine how we frame things. From studying core beliefs, you begin to sense the vastness of how these thought patterns permeate our lives.

Now that you have gathered a collection of your own beliefs take stock of them. Which are helpful? Which cause problems? Perhaps you were startled to find certain limiting beliefs that you carry. It is part of the human experience. Take a deep breath now and know you have tools - the 5 Steps - to change those restrictive thought patterns. Affirm your growth and know you are on a path to wholeness.

The children in our lives reflect back our own beliefs. Sometimes we impart our views to the younger generation. By overcoming our own limitations, we help both ourselves and the children we touch. We can all progress together with our liberating beliefs.

Remember, this appendix is a resource. Over time you can review this belief inventory and see how much you have grown. By using the 5 Steps you create more possibilities for yourself. You can use Appendix F to journal on any problems and off beliefs you have encountered.

Examples of On and Off Beliefs

This appendix offers you a sampling of different beliefs as a reference. The beliefs listed are not definitive and many variations exist. The previous Appendix C on "Discovering Different Core Beliefs" can help you identify other outlooks. A collection of beliefs form a belief system, which creates attitudes.

 People, particularly developing children, collect and hold beliefs, acquiring them from parents and other authority figures, peers, and media. You can carry off beliefs for as long as a lifetime if left unexamined.

Notice how the off beliefs show an I am more than or less than others viewpoint, having the person feel separated and at odds with himself and others. By contrast, the on beliefs honor the person's uniqueness, allowing him respect for self and others. As you know, the 5 Steps switches off beliefs to on beliefs.

TABLE D
COMPARISON OF ON AND OFF BELIEFS

Off Belief	On Belief
1) School work is hard.	I can improve.
2) If I ask for help, I'm stupid.	I learn by asking for help.
3) I can't stand people criticizing me.	I can handle criticism.
4) I have to get what I want.	I can live without it.
5) Things are unfair.	Things are fair. I can make things fairer. I can handle it when things are unfair.
6) Nobody likes me.	Some people like me.
7) I must be perfect.	I can learn from mistakes.
8) That person makes me angry.	I am responsible for what I feel and think, and for how I behave.
9) Lying gets you out of trouble.	I tell the truth. I can be more honest.
10) I have to do it this way.	I can do it different ways.

Getting *thru* Visualization

Visualization is one of the mind's primary ways to express itself. As mentioned previously, we continuously image our world through experiences, dreams, creativity, and communication. You can heal yourself and draw positive pictures to yourself if you choose. By relaxing, you experience subtle and profound change through visualization.

The following creative visualization was inspired by Madonna Polley, C.H.T. You can use this exercise with any problem to prepare yourself for the 5 Steps, as either a facilitator or recipient of the process. You can also do this visualization after the 5 Steps to deepen or reinforce the learning. You might want to listen to it with the child.

Find a relaxed position in a comfortable chair or lie down. Arrange to have privacy during this visualization. You can have a friend read you the meditation, record it onto a tape, read it in parts to yourself or memorize the gist of it.

Become more and more comfortable as you feel yourself sitting or lying down.... Notice your breathing. Count down from ten to one and with each number relax more deeply.... Let go of any tension in the body.... Keep breathing slowly and deeply, letting go more with every breath. That's it, relaxing as you have so many times before, in just the right way for you... (pause for a moment before going on to the next paragraph).

Now begin to sense or see yourself in a natural environment, near a beautiful lake or stream.... Gently go towards the water as you take in the beauty of the surroundings, so safe and peaceful. Looking into the water you see your reflection. Notice how it looks, study its features.... (pause)

Now ask the reflection about the problem you have. Listen carefully and allow the response to come to you... Have the reflection mirror your feelings about the problem. Note the particular shape of the face as the emotions reflect back to you.... Now ask the reflection what it thinks about the problem and the feelings that have been created? Listen for any beliefs that surface from the watery source... (pause)

As the belief becomes clarified, you may see a scene within the water.... Ask the watery guide how to change the belief... opening and releasing into a more positive state. Watch and listen closely... (pause)

Now ask the watery image to foretell a positive future, based on the new understanding and belief you received. Take in all the images, sounds, and feelings you experience. Notice the new welcome color(s) of this positive future. (pause)

Thank the watery reflection and listen for any final messages. Realize that you can return to this resourceful haven whenever you wish. You can use whatever you choose from this experience and disregard anything as well....

Now it's time to return to the room. Start moving your arms and legs, preparing to come back refreshed, alert, and ready to continue with your day. Counting from one to five: one... two... three... four, getting ready to open your eyes... and five! Eyes wide open and feeling wonderful...

Going Deeper by Using a 5 Step Journal

Use your notebook to explore your own problems and beliefs. Journalling will deepen the experience so you know yourself better. This will be a great benefit when you work with kids using the same process.

Just allow space in your notebook for each part of the process. If you want an overview, see Chapter Eight, "A Quick Reference to the 5 Steps."

STEP 1: *Identify the problem.*

STEP 2: *Identify the feelings* about the problem. Look for a restrictive belief, the "off belief." (There may be more than one limiting belief.)

STEP 3: *Look for a restrictive belief,* the off belief. By expressing your feelings and thoughts on the situation, a distorted belief will surface. (There may be more than one off belief connected with the situation.)

STEP 4: *Find a new belief,* one that is more opening, embracing, enhancing, and freeing, the "on belief." You can help shift your belief by playing "Truth," "Consequences" or "Change." (Refer to the section "On Belief" if you want to review these approaches.)

STEP 5: *Imagine your future* with the new belief installed. Use your senses to describe the sights, sounds, sensations, feelings, tastes, and aromas if possible.

Troubleshooting: If the future is not as positive as you wish, review step three or four of the process. Did you identify the off belief correctly (step three)? Did you find a suitable on belief, and state it in the positive without absolutes (step four)? You can also brighten up this future vision by enhancing colors, changing sounds or volumes and enhancing feelings, sensations, tastes, and aromas.

Review and take stock of what you have written. You may find keys that can unlock many new possibilities. And as you go through the 5 Steps for yourself, you increase the chances of growth for those around you. Getting thru to kids has a lot to do with getting thru to yourself. Congratulations on the steps you have taken.

Selected Bibliography

Alberti, R., and M. Emmons. *Stand Up, Speak Out, Talk Back!*
New York: Pocket Books, 1975.

Anderson, Jill. *Thinking, Changing, Rearranging.* Portland,
Oregon: Metamorphous Press, 1988.

Bayard R., and J. Bayard. *How to Deal with Your Acting-Up
Teenager.* New York: M. Evans & Company, Inc., 1983.

Bishop, J., and M. Grunte. *How to Forgive When You Don't
Know How.* New York: Station Hill Press, 1993.

Elium D., and J. Elium. *Raising A Son.* Hillsboro, Oregon:
Beyond Words Publishing, 1992.

Ellis A., and A. Lange. *How To Keep People From Pushing Your
Buttons.* Birch Lane Press, 1994.

Faber, A., and E. Mazlish. *How To Talk So Kids Will Listen &
Listen So Kids Will Talk.* New York: Avon Books, 1982.

Ferrini, Paul. *The Silence of the Heart.* Heartways Press, PO
Box 181, So. Deerfield, MA 01373, 1996.

Goleman, Daniel. *Emotional Intelligence.* New York: Bantam
Books, 1995.

James, J., and F. Cherry. *The Grief Recovery Handbook.* New
York: Harper Perennial, 1988.

McKay, M., and P. Fanning. *Prisoners of Belief.* Oakland,
California: New Harbinger Publications, 1991.

_____. *Self-Esteem*. Oakland, California:
New Harbinger Publications, 1987.

Nye, Budd. *Understanding and Managing Your Anger and
Aggression*. Federal Way, Washington, 1993.

Rosenblatt, Roger. "The Society that Pretends to Love
Children." New York Times Magazine, 8 October 1995,
58-61.

Stone, H., and S. Winkelman. *Embracing Each Other*. San
Rafael, California: New World Library, 1989.

_____. *Embracing Our Selves*. San Rafael,
California: New World Library, 1989.

Taylor, Cathryn L. *The Inner Child Workbook*. New York: G.P.
Putnam's Sons, 1991.

Index

About the Author

Phillip Mountrose has been educating kids of all ages for over twenty years. He has a Masters in Education from Boston State College, a Special Education Certification, and a Masters in Fine Arts and TV Production from UCLA. Phillip has taught K-12 classes, including special education with emotionally disturbed adolescents. His inspiring instructional videos specialize in improving work attitudes for youth. They are used in school districts nationwide. Phillip has developed an innovative approach from working for many years with individuals and groups in the area of self-help.

For information about scheduling personal sessions, consultations, speaking engagements, and seminars contact:

Phillip Mountrose
P.O. Box 41152
Sacramento, CA 95841-0152
fax: 916-972-0237
E-mail: getthru@jps.net
www.jps.net/holistic/getthru.html

Take Advantage of these Audiotapes

Getting Thru to Kids:
Problem-Solving with Children Ages 6 to 18.

This two-tape audio set gives you the essence of the book, read by the author with dramatized readings from the transcriptions in the manual. Uplifting and easy, great for deepening your communication skills. $16.95

The Holistic Approach to Eating:
How To Easily Let Go of Extra Weight
and Keep It Off For Life!

This two-tape set with supplementary manual gives you the keys to losing and maintaining your weight for life! Learn the reasons traditional diets fail and techniques that really work. Make real progress and feel good about yourself. Narrated and authored by veteran hypnotherapist Jane Mountrose, these engaging tapes and manual teach you natural ways to lasting success. $24.95

Complete money-back guarantee!

Order Form

ITEM	QUANTITY	COST
Getting *Thru* to Kids: book $11.95	____	_____
Getting *Thru* to Kids: 2 audio tapes $16.95	____	_____
The Holistic Approach to Eating: 2 audio tapes and supplementary manual $24.95	____	_____

Subtotal _____

Shipping: $3.00 first item, $1.00 each additional item   _____

California residents please add 7.75% for sales tax   _____

AMOUNT ENCLOSED _____

Ship to:

Name: _____

Company: _____

Address: _____

City:_____State: _____

Zip: _____Phone:(_____)_____

Payment: ___ Check   ___ Money Order   ___ Credit Card:

___ Visa,   ___ Mastercard   ___ Discover

Card Number _____

Name on card:_____

Expiration Date: _____/_____

Mail to: Holistic Communications,
PO Box 41152 Dept B, Sacramento, CA 95841-0152

Fax orders: (916) 972-0237

TOLL FREE **24 Hour Order Line:** (800)644-KIDS

Money Back Guarantee!

Order Form

ITEM	QUANTITY	COST
Getting *Thru* to Kids: book $11.95	____	_____
Getting *Thru* to Kids: 2 audio tapes $16.95	____	_____
The Holistic Approach to Eating: 2 audio tapes and supplementary manual $24.95	____	_____
Subtotal		_____
Shipping: $3.00 first item, $1.00 each additional item		_____
California residents please add 7.75% for sales tax		_____
AMOUNT ENCLOSED		_____

Ship to:

Name: _____

Company: _____

Address: _____

City:_____State: _____

Zip: _____Phone:(_____)_____

Payment: ___ Check   ___ Money Order   ___ Credit Card:

___ Visa,   ___ Mastercard   ___ Discover

Card Number _____

Name on card:_____

Expiration Date: _____/_____

Mail to: Holistic Communications,
              PO Box 41152 Dept B, Sacramento, CA 95841-0152

Fax orders: (916) 972-0237

TOLL FREE **24 Hour Order Line:** (800)644-KIDS

Money Back Guarantee!